SEEKING PURPOSE

THE QUESTIONS WE WOULD LIKE TO ASK, BUT SOCIETY SAYS WE CAN'T

Robert Zadkiel Young

ISBN 979-8-89243-267-2 (paperback)
ISBN 979-8-89243-268-9 (digital)

Christian Faith Publishing
832 Park Avenue
Meadville, PA 16335
www.christianfaithpublishing.com

Printed in the United States of America

Contents

Introduction

To all who read these words, peace be on to you. All over the world, there are people who have gone, and still are going through, so much suffering. This book was created with that understanding alone. For those who are hurting inside, troubled by thoughts of guilt from past mistakes: Hold on and be strong. You are not alone!

Life is a test that many have failed. We all seek answers to questions we cannot understand. But the most important thing is that you realize you should never give up. Never give up on searching for truth and your purpose in life! Signs are all around us. Just open your eyes, and you will see them.

Seeking purpose is the whole idea! Bruce Lee once said, "I do not pray for an easy life! I pray to gain the strength to endure a hard life."

So never give up, never walk with your head down! Seeking purpose isn't a test—it's life!

The Questions

Many years ago, I came across a Bible verse which disturbed me still to this day. I would like to share it with you.

> For I know the thoughts that I have towards
> you, saith the lord.
> Thoughts of peace, and not of evil, to give
> you an expected end. (Jeremiah 29:11 KJV)

Take a moment to consider this quote. I had reached a pivotal point in my life in which I yearned to transform my life for the better. One day I was studying in the Holy Bible and unintentionally stumbled over this verse that would change my life. It's very funny how, when you're searching for answers, you tend to find the very thing you actually need instead.

Many nights I would ponder on whether this was true. At that moment, I was very down and felt as if I was cursed, doomed to fulfill this prophecy called life with no hope of a positive future. *Was I only here to peacefully prepare for an expected end without purpose?* The unknown can be alluring but, at the same time, remarkably terrifying. I was seeking my own purpose in life because I felt I had none.

Have you ever felt this way? Have you ever found yourself questioning God on why he even created you, or even us? I was so fixated on the belief that maybe, just maybe, I was worth more than an experimental lab mouse, trapped in a cage to be used against my will. My free will. It felt as if God Himself was punishing me for something I was unaware of participating in. What an extremely uncomfortable experience.

This verse constantly replayed in my mind. Then something hit me like a baseball bat in the head, shocking me to the core. Maybe having faith in a Creator whom I've never seen wasn't the problem. Maybe the lack of faith in myself was the problem. Right at that very moment, a thought struck me like a lightning bolt.

How is ending my life, in any way, shape, or form, peaceful?

This made me study intensely. Maybe I was wrong. Maybe I took the content out of context! So I began to research this quote using other versions of the Bible, hoping to gain more clarity. My secondary source was the ESV (English Standard Version). This version of the Bible reproduces the precise wording of the original text in a modern mainstream English-standard translation, making it easier for individuals like me to understand. Just as I hoped for, success!

> For I know the plans I have for you, declares
> the Lord, plans for welfare[1] and not for evil, to
> give you a future and a hope. (Jeremiah 29:11)

Sounds much better, wouldn't you agree? See, when you study the Holy Bible, you must be aware of the origins of the information it contains. The individuals who witnessed it and lived back then spoke a language different from ours. They had a different lifestyle. This meant the events and stories that were depicted differ from our understanding as well. In addition, to understand this vital point, you must also be aware that these verses may also contain hidden, encrypted messages that must be deciphered correctly for proper understanding in this, their future. The Scriptures do warn us about this.

> For in much wisdom is much grief: and
> he that increaseth knowledge increaseth sorrow.
> (Ecclesiastes 1:18 KJV)

---

[1]   Also means "peace" (biblegateway.com)

For in much wisdom is much vexation, and
he who increases knowledge increases sorrow.
(Ecclesiastes 1:18 ESV)

Definition of *vexation*: "the quality or state of being vexed; irritation; a cause of trouble; affliction; the act of harassing; troubling" (*Merriam-Webster's Collegiate Dictionary*).

Now as I continued to analyze the differences in the meanings, the realization of this mysterious quote became clearer to me. It wasn't necessarily referring to just death but a completion of a cycle in our life. Like all things in our lives, there is a beginning and end. So if we look at the text from a logical standpoint, we notice the Scripture is expressing that God wants us to live with a purpose instead of dying without one. *How would you feel knowing you lived all these years on this earth and, when it's your time to face your end, you look back and realize it was all for nothing?*

More so, in a sense, the verse referred to both living and dying in the same words, just with a purpose. As we all know, death is inevitable; so if God's wish for us was to have hope and not suffer evil in this life, then we must ask ourselves what is worth living and dying for in this life. Stay with me here. My point will soon make sense.

Follow me as we embark on this journey down a rabbit hole to several other questions I ponder about. Much of my life found myself indulging in numerous books which would cover many other subjects' basis, such as philosophers, war and peace, self-development, ancient civilizations, spiritual practices and rituals, warriors' beliefs, marriages and relationships, hidden discoveries found in the world, etc.

Let me first take a quick moment to explain why I was such a curious individual so you can grasp the intensity of my thought process and why I was such a voracious reader. I was looking for something. I just wasn't sure what.

I was born in the early '80s. Growing up in that era, much of my influences were self-exposure based. I grew up in the era of the Black Panthers and civil rights movements. This was the pinnacle of drugs and gang violence in America, war on political injustice, and the heightened hysteria of religion believers who seemed to fuss and fight over whose facts were correct about God. Much of what I've mentioned is now, unfortunately, still occurring today.

Being raised as an only child in a dysfunctional home with the lack of a father in the household to teach me how to become a man, and an unbalanced mother who suffered abandonment issues caused by an absent family, I had no sense of real direction. Like most broke kids with self-esteem issues, I clung to the streets. The gang life, fast lifestyle, drug dealers, and pimps were my idols and caretakers. This was the environment of my youth. It helped direct my path to becoming a man. Well, at least that's how I felt. The crazy part about this was, many of them were educated and made sure I stayed in school no matter what.

Divine Intervention

When I was around four years old, before my life would have changed completely, God decided to expose me to my first encounter with death. This would be my first divine intervention experience.

Definition of *divine intervention*: "An event that occurs when a deity becomes actively involved in changing some situation in human affairs."

One day, I was heading to church with a family member and her daughters. I remember this day being the worst day of my life, even though I was just a small child. No one could have known what was going to occur. We were all involved in a terrible car crash. I was flung from the backseat of the car, headfirst, straight into and through the windshield. A large piece of windshield glass plunged directly into my head. Once the paramedics arrived on the scene, someone pronounced me dead.

Lying there face down with my backside up, covered in my own blood mixed with pieces of shattered glass everywhere, no movement was seen. I was just a lifeless body, absent of a soul, laid on top of the front hood of the vehicle.

There is an old saying found to be true:

God doesn't make any mistakes; his will be done!

Well, I guess that was correct. God wasn't finished with me. One of the medics persisted and would not give up on me. Repeatedly, he tried to resuscitate me. Just when that medic had finally accepted that this was the end for the little guy (me), a little breath of air flowed through my lungs, and I started breathing again.

I found all this out years ago, when I got older, from my mother. FYI: I did have my seat belt on, she told me, but no one could explain the miraculous event. Somehow, out of everyone else in the car, I was the only one who suffered the worst. Everyone else suffered cuts and bruises. Oh, don't worry, I'll say it for you!

How in the hell was I the only one so badly injured?

Yeah. Many nights, I pondered this question as well. It just didn't make sense to me. Now can you understand what I mentioned earlier? I was feeling as if my life was cursed. Let that sink in now! All things must come to an end to welcome in the new. My life ended at the tender age of four years old.

When I came out of the hospital, I was healed, but for a kid my age, the healing process made me feel alone. A traumatic experience was suffered by a four-year-old child. I felt alone and frightened, but I learned how to suppress my feelings even at that tender age. I changed.

After I came home, I started noticing that I was speaking differently. I was more mature. I started questioning my mother about things I'd never mentioned before. I was a serious child asking spiritual questions that she had no answers to. My mother knew something had changed. I'd never asked questions about God before.

She asked me where I was getting these questions from. She asked me what happened to me because of the way I was able to articulate myself and was no longer a four- or five-year-old kid. I had become an old soul. I was comprehending things and changed the way I spoke. She no longer had answers for me. I was different. I became lonely. My mother and the other family members thought I'd become mysterious. Others avoided me. My mom was the only person I had left.

When I got older and started working, I felt obliged to start taking care of my mother. She was my mother. She stood by me. I grew up fast. I started working at the age of thirteen years. I didn't have much of a childhood, at least not one you could call enjoyable. When I wasn't working, I would stay in my room for hours and keep to myself. I didn't want to be on the streets all the time, so I spent the majority of my time in that room. I found answers but still felt cursed. It was a way for me to get away from the world, losing myself in my room.

Sure, I would go out and have some fun sometimes, but the majority of the time was in my room with my punching bag and books. I'd practice martial arts and read poetry. Even though I hid myself away, I still considered my mom my best friend, and I was hers. That's how we survived.

I began to look up to the neighborhood drug dealers and other men in other businesses. I looked up to them because they were all around. They'd become my male role models. By the time I was sixteen years old, I was making some pretty good money, enough to help pay the bills. I held a job and went to school. My role models made sure I stayed in school. They looked after me to keep me safe and made sure we were fed. I changed a little, but I never became one of them. I realized that if I didn't get out of there, I was going to be stuck.

The opportunity came, and I joined the Marines, even though I thought I hated the military. I did my research first. It was my chance to get out of that neighborhood and make a better way for myself and my mom. It was almost like I had another divine intervention. The chance came, and I went. I didn't even tell mom. I left when the recruiter came to pick me up at three o'clock in the morning, and two days later, I called her from Paris Island.

It's almost like the Holy Spirit went into me when I died. He just let me be a kid and ask the right questions and protected me until it was time to put me where I needed to be. I feel like I can be a spiritual teacher now, deep in the spirituality of learning about myself, about God, about life. It wasn't about me going to church. Again, it was a way for me to get away from the world.

My experience was a double-edged sword. As I grew older, the sense of being alone no longer bothered me. In fact, I grew fond of it very much. Hiding my emotions became easy. I could smile straight in your face and be extremely mad all at the same time. As much as I was shown love, it didn't matter to me. I accepted the dark more than the light. The world became unfamiliar to me, and I felt I never belonged here.

Relationships with women were never fulfilling. Conflict with people never bothered me. In fact, I loved it. I was bullied by my friends and foes alike. But somehow, I managed to develop a really tough exterior. Books still attracted me, and with them, I found some sense of peace. I was forced into my own world to gain a sense of what real self-development consisted of, but I was still a walking time bomb, waiting to erupt at any given time.

I've changed a lot since then, but my attitude was still there. Living in my own head was my safe spot. Everything outside of it was just hell. The more aggressively I studied, the more aggressive I became for trying to figure out my life. Something was just unsettling with me about this world, and I wanted to know why! God had given me a strong spirit and a second chance at life, so I wasn't going to waste it.

All Grown-Up?

Years passed by, and now I was living life on my own terms.

In 2008, when I joined the United States Marine Corp, I found it a totally different world than what I was used to. It was fast, harsh, structured, and everyone I knew felt the Marines was the best branch and the toughest to get into. Right up my area. Hell, if you're going to shoot for the stars, why not learn from the best and with a gun to do so.

Still, after serving four combat tours in Afghanistan, plus life situations, again my outlook on life changed. My mission now in life is to uplift and teach others about how to see life in a different manner. I used my pain, past experiences, and all the wisdom gathered from studying life to influence change in the mind, body, and spirit. God be praised. He helped me develop a unique way to help individuals who lack understanding of self-worth, faith, and personal ideas to invoke change in their lives. Being lost in the dark isn't always a bad thing.

Some of God's works, if not all, were done in the dark in a unique way to discover and excel in figuring out their own purpose. Many believe they can't escape the dark. Well, I'm here to prove that myth wrong! We speak on faith like it's something freely given. I believe that is absolutely wrong. It must be earned. The only requirement is, you must be willing to sacrifice yourself to achieve it. Nothing is free in this life, only God's divine love.

We are living in a world in which the certainty of dying is more relevant than living. We tend to mimic each other with no sense of direction on how to create our own identity. This must stop.

Without God in your life, all hope is lost. My experiences and wisdom endured in this journey called life may seem unorthodox, but I promise relevance now.

It's time we gain a new understanding about faith and life. God be praised; many are doing so. Now here's a new version from someone chosen to do so as well. Feel free to judge me. Just know I have every right to judge you back as well. We are all aware there can be only one true judge at the end. Our king, Lord Jesus Christ, son of God Almighty, YAHAWA, ALLAH, ELOHIM. This generation knows of him by many names. I simply refer to him as DAD!

God made me different. So here I am in all of God's majesty. Achieving your dreams will always be the goal in this life, but have you ever considered that all the spoils of life are only temporary? We can't take anything with us when it's our time to leave this earth, but we can take the wisdom gained here on earth and the faith earned knowing that *we were not a mistake*! Now enough about me, let's continue down this rabbit hole.

Homework

You will find throughout this book, blank pages or partial pages, for you to share your own story. In fact, there is extra room after each major question for you to call to mind your own opinions and realizations. This book is meant to provoke your thoughts on the matters I present. Take a moment to reflect on your life's beginnings.

- How did you get where you are right now?
- Who or what do you feel influenced you to make the decisions you have made in your life?

The following blank pages are for you to tell your own story.

The Process

Now, if your attention span isn't too short, then you have made it with me so far on this journey. Unlike most fairy tales that depict the main character awakening on the other side, take into consideration that this hole is dark, and you're still inside. What's inside may still scare you, but you're on your way out. You won't face this alone. The spirit will guide you along the way. So let us continue our exploration together on understanding yourself. Fear not, God is with you, and so am I.

There's a poem that pretty much sums up everything. Have you ever read the poem "Footprints in the Sand," written by Mary Stevenson? What an inspiring piece of heartfelt work! Thank you, Mrs. Stevenson, for sharing your light with us. By far, in my opinion, this poem should be placed in the archives amongst the greatest collections of rare, raw, historical, land-breaking documents, forever protected.

Footprints in the Sand
Mary Stevenson

One night I dreamed a dream
As I was walking along the beach with my Lord.
Across the dark sky flashed scenes from my life.
For each scene, I noticed two sets of footprints
    in the sand,
one belonging to me and one to my Lord.
After the last scene of my life flashed before me,

I looked back at the footprints in the sand.
I noticed that at many times along the path of
     my life,
especially at the very lowest and saddest times,
there was only one set of footprints.
This really troubled me, so I asked the Lord
     about it.
"Lord, you said once I decided to follow you,
you'd walk with me all the way.
But I noticed that during the saddest and most
     troublesome times of my life,
there was only one set of footprints.
I don't understand why, when I needed you the
     most, you would leave me."
He whispered, "My precious child, I love you
     and will never leave you
never, ever, during your trials and testing's.
When you saw only one set of footprints,
it was then that I carried you.

Faith, Hope, and Moses

All my life, I've always noticed that the individuals who indulged in endless evil endeavors, committing heinous crimes, seem to always flourish while gaining the respect and praises of the masses.

Meanwhile, the hard-working common men/women break their backs just to receive backlash for thinking outside the box. Still, they carry on with the hope of gaining a little freedom. Have you ever noticed that? I would wonder, *God, do you care that all of this is killing us?*

Many nights I would torture myself because I was aware of this pain and confusion we are in. Completely depleted from overthinking, all I could comprehend was that it made me extremely tired and scared of my own reflection in the mirror. Depressed and unsatisfied with my own life, I would find myself just sitting in the dark, crying and asking God, "Why me, Lord? Why did you bring me back to this life?"

Every time I took a step forward in my life, I found myself taking two steps backward. Praying for death to come and take me back became a daily ritual for me. A very depressing and overwhelming feeling comes over you anytime you think like this. Realization of this occurs when you step back and analyze your life only to discover you really have no way out. You see, there is no one to rely on but yourself to fight back. When I realized I had not accomplished anything in my life worth being proud about, it made me just want to give up and bail out.

Not understanding why, but for some reason, I began to reflect on the story of Moses in the Holy Bible. Moses was an abandoned child whose family felt he was better off without them. If you can relate to that scenario, then you will understand where I'm going with this. If you are unfamiliar with Moses's story, then I will share it with you. It might become clear that Moses's story was of a betrayal like I had mentioned, but I couldn't help but think why his mother didn't choose another path to save him. Why leave it to chance if you have faith in the Creator?

The story of Moses was very strange but surprisingly uplifting all at the same time to me. There were many mysterious twists and turns of dilemmas he had to face along the journey to become the deliverer of his people and God's instrument of wrath. In some of my lowest moments, I couldn't help but ponder, *Does God just use us as sacrificial lambs to the slaughter, or does he use us to exercise his power on his enemies or both?* When you hear the whole story of Moses, think about those questions.

I know that they are such extremely harsh questions to ask, but I was in a very low vibration at the time. As perplexing as Moses's situation was, somehow it still led him to achieve the prophetic blessing that would change the narrative of many lives. The story of Moses shows us that our past does influence our futures. But if we accept knowing this, we can still use the experiences gathered along our journey, flipping it and developing our futures correctly—differently than what we had previously anticipated.

Moses is considered and revered as the greatest prophet and teacher in the Holy Bible. A child born of Hebrew parents from the tribe of Levi, Moses's life was completely a real manifestation to behold, thoroughly designed by God himself. Here was a savior trapped in a little child's body. He had no clue about what he was destined to become.

His story begins with his mother hearing word that the Pharaoh of Egypt had tasked out his entire army in hopes to kill every newborn boy child. Why? Because he feared that the Hebrews would one day rise up and overpower him. Moses's mother hid her newborn son (Moses) for three whole months just to save his life.

Realizing she could no longer keep him safe by herself, she placed Moses in a basket made of reeds and placed the makeshift boat in the Nile River to set sail for safety; she prayed. She was hoping, having faith, that God would protect her son from Pharoah Ramsey's wrath.

Definition of *reeds*: "A tall, slender-leaved plant of the grass family, which grows in water or on marshy grounds."

Now pause for a second please. Let me clarify something quick. A lot of people today still confuse hope versus faith being one in the same—not so.

The definition of *hope* is "a feeling of *expectation and desire* for a certain thing to happen," while the definition of *faith* is "*complete trust* or confidence in someone or something."

Do you understand the difference?

Now that we got that straightened out, let's continue where we left off. Floating along the rough water of the Nile River was a lonely basket containing what many would say to be a miracle child. The basket reached the banks of the Pharaoh's palace, and who's there, bathing? The Pharoah's daughter and her Hebrew slave maid.

That's right. I forgot to mention, while on the quest to kill all the Hebrews, many of the newborn children were slaughtered; but as a token to his own people, the Pharaoh allowed the rest of the men and women to live as slaves under his power. The women were made house slaves to be used at Ramsey's beck and call.

Back to the story now. The Pharaoh's daughter notices the basket floating by in the river. Curious to know what's inside she instructed her maid to retrieve the basket.

She was amazed to see a child inside. But it was not just any old regular child—it was a newborn boy Hebrew child. The daughter then decided to keep the child, not mentioning it to her father (Pharaoh) but instead hiding the child as if it were a found puppy she might not be allowed to keep. Do you now understand what I meant earlier? These twists and turns of Moses's life were designed.

Doesn't it remind you of the action done by Moses's mother? Now we notice the daughter reacting in the same fashion to protect Moses yet again. The crazy part of this story was that the daughter of Pharoah was the one who gave Moses his name, and not the real mother. Now get ready, let me quarter back this ideal game plan out for you. Let me show you the genius mind of the God we serve because without knowledge of this, you won't get my whole point of why God led me to thinking about this particular story at the time. I was questioning my past, present, and future.

Definition of the name Moses: "The name Moses is primarily a male name of Egyptian origin that means 'born of a God' or 'drew out.'" The name Moses also means (in Hebrew) "drew out."

Now watch the master planner at work. Don't ever tell yourself again, "God isn't real, and there's no plan for your life ever again!"

Without knowledge that the Lord is going to use this daughter of Pharaoh, she gave the child a name, Moses, which would not just conceal Moses's past but at the same time save his future. When the daughter finally introduced the child to her father, he asked her the child's name. She replied, "Moses, Father."

Pharoah, now pleased in seeing the child for the very first time, insisted that he would grow up alongside his first male child, baby Ramsey. If only he did his research on the name, he would have known the name given to the child represents both Egyptian and Hebrew descent. Why is this important? The same generation of people he had desired to eradicate from existence, he instead enslaved. One of them was now living in his palace to be raised and protected by him.

Two princes of Egypt, whose birth right differs from one another, were now able to fight for the future legacy. Who would win—the Egyptians or Hebrews? Moses, unaware of this future dilemma, was given a name in which God would use to unlock his past, one day in the present, just to fulfill God's plans for his future. The very curse the Pharoah had spoken in an attempt to save his status would not only backfire on him for what he had done to God's people but also destroy his own son's future. The given name, Moses, was not only the key but also the weapon of God's wrath.

Take this into consideration. If you knew God's thoughts, you would never question God on why he allows the things you must go through in life. Some pain is greater than you think you can handle. I understand this, but if you survived, what would that make you? The path to become who you were meant to become is different from everyone else's path. I didn't understand this at that time. The difference between God's blessings and the devil's manipulations? God does all his best work behind the scenes in the dark, while the devil seeks the glory posing as the light.

> For my thoughts are not your thoughts, neither are your ways my ways, saith the LORD.
> For as the heavens are higher than the earth, so are my ways higher than your ways, and my thoughts than your thoughts. (Isaiah 55:8–9 KJV)

> For my thoughts are not your thoughts, neither are your ways my ways, declares the LORD.
> For as the heavens are higher than the earth, so are my ways higher than your ways and my thoughts than your thoughts. (Isaiah 55:8–9 ESV)

(Oh, that is some cold blooded sh—well, it just seemed mean.)

Sorry. I won't spill the whole Moses story here. You must read it yourself. Trust me, it gets good. Now doesn't this seem familiar, constantly facing an identity crisis. Hidden lies told to us every day by society, parents, and others whom we entrust. All we desire is the truth of who we are. In my opinion, if you want to know the truth, you have got to find it out yourself. I was so upset knowing this outrage I began cursing his name.

> Ye shall not go after other gods, of the gods of the people which are round about you;
> For the LORD thy God is a jealous God among you lest the anger of the LORD thy God be kindled against thee and destroy thee from off the face of the earth.
> Ye shall not tempt the LORD your God, as ye tempted him in Massah. (Deuteronomy 6:14–16 KJV)

> You shall not go after other gods, the gods of the peoples who are around you, For the LORD your God in your midst is a jealous God—lest the anger of the LORD your God be kindled against you, and he destroys you from off the face of the earth. You shall not put the LORD your God to the test, as you tested him at Massah." (Deuteronomy 6:14–16)

(Other gods nowadays could even mean "influencers"—influencers of social media, actors, so-called friends that do not lift you up.)

My behavior became reckless, rebellious toward God, until one day I, yet again, remembered this story of Moses. When I could no longer feel God's presence around me, it scared me. Vacillation can change a person completely. We must learn how to become humble and trust the process of change. Learning how to love yourself and understand your own self-worth is very important. Too many of us still rely on codependency, needing someone else to validate you.

To establish what we consider to be our true selves in this lifetime, we need to stop asking blind people to tell us our futures. We are giving away too much power to them who simply care only to use it against us. This weakness goes against our reciprocity in which we need to succeed in this life. You do not need permission to grow. The pain and hurt you will have to endure will do that all on its own. Accept it.

If your struggles cause others to forget you, then your strength will cause them to remember you. When we learn the art of integrity, taking full responsibility of our actions are more likely to occur. In fact, it's a major requirement for self-healing. This is the process we all must consistently work on. It's okay to cry and shed your tears of discontent but understand something: your tantrums can easily be misread as actions of disobedience. We shouldn't fear the inability to understand why our lives are the way they are but instead embrace it, because it will force you to want to discover its origin. We need to ask God the right questions so he can direct our steps accordingly.

The following article has shone so much light on my life I wanted to share it with you. Maybe it will shed light on your life as well.

Our Deepest Fear
Marianna Williamson

Our deepest fear is not that we are inadequate. Our deepest fear is that we are powerful beyond measure. It is our light, not our darkness, that most frightens us. We ask ourselves, who am I to be brilliant, gorgeous, talented, and fabulous? Actually, who are you not to be? You are a child of God. Your "playing small" does not serve the world. There is nothing enlightened about shrinking so that other people won't feel insecure around you.

We are all meant to shine, as children do. We were born to make manifest the glory of God that is within us. It's not just in some of us, it's in everyone. And as we let our own light shine, we unconsciously give other people permission to do

the same. As we are liberated from our own fear,
our presence automatically liberates others.

Manifestation requires the sacrifice of all your hidden agendas. Negative thoughts are portent black clouds of disbeliefs that can kill any dreams. The hardest lesson in life, in my opinion, is figuring out your self-worth. People claim to understand you, but when you change and it's noticeable, that's when they begin to hate you. Mature individuals don't follow the pack; they're the ones leading the pack. Hate them or love them, they were the ones who decided to stand out and not fit in.

You have to decide right here and now about what you are going to do with your life. Be careful of what you tolerate in your life. We tend to teach people how to manipulate us.

In the late 1800s, an Indian philosopher, by the name of Jiddu Krishnamurti, once said, "It is the truth that liberates, not your effort to be free" (TruthUltimate.com). Some might vary the sentence structure, but it still means the same: "It is the truth, not your efforts to be free, that liberate." We will visit his thoughts again later.

The idea of knowing you are special is worth protecting. Change must occur for you to learn. Life is chess, not checkers. Every move you make must be intentional and accurate. Life is the opponent on the opposite side of the board, unphased by your decisions yet always calculating your next few moves. Life will move what you may consider weak pieces in front of you just to draw you out, leaving you exposed. You will be wide open to a power move, then checkmate.

Do you know why the story of the turtle and the hare is so significant to folks like me? If you are not familiar with the tale, or *Aesop's Fables*, I will share it with you here. The fables were known as moral character-building lessons passed down from generation to generation.

The Tortoise and the Hare

The story is about, of course, a tortoise and a hare. A tortoise is a very slow-moving creature, a turtle, if you will. A hare is a type of rabbit, quick and agile.

The Hare was always teasing the Tortoise about being slow until the Tortoise challenged the Hare to a race.

The Hare, of course, laughed but accepted the challenge. The Fox would set up the course and judge who won at the end.

The Hare left the Tortoise behind from the start. He was so far ahead of the Tortoise he decided to take a nap halfway through the course. He figured that the Tortoise was so far behind he would never catch up.

While the Hare planned a nap, he ended up fast asleep as the Tortoise kept plodding along, slowly but steadily.

The Hare woke up and was a bit annoyed that he had actually fallen fast asleep.

He got up and raced toward the finish line as fast as he could, but he was too late.

The Tortoise had already won.

There was a valuable lesson to be learned about that situation. You can be the fastest runner in this race called life, but in the end, slow and steady will always win the race. *Why?* Because it doesn't make any sense to finish first and lack the energy to run again, when you can be patient and take your time, conserving energy to race again another day if needed.

Here are some *review questions*. There are no wrong answers. This is a guide to help you reflect on your own image, mind, and heart.

- Use the following pages to enter your own opinions, thoughts, feelings, or translations to the points already mentioned.
- Read "Footprints in the Sand" again. How do you feel when you are feeling down and alone?

- Do you feel like God is trying to kill us because we have to work so hard to get anywhere when others do evil and get ahead? How and why?

- Read the fable about "The Tortoise and the Hare" again. Compare your work life to the story. Have you ever been racing around, trying to get to a goal first, just to find that someone who was not particularly special, who stayed quiet with his nose to the grindstone, got to the goal first? How did it make you feel? What did you learn?

- I know why now, but why do you think I was brought back from the dead? What would you be feeling if it was you that returned from the other side?

- Do you think God wants us as sacrificial lambs, and to what end?

- Do you think he uses us to exercise power over his enemies? How?

- Have you ever seen crabs in a bucket and noticed how when one makes it to the top to escape, the others start pulling it back in? Are they trying to stop its escape or use it to pull themselves up? Can you apply the same scenario to your life?

- Will you take full responsibility for all your actions and mistakes?

- When has the truth set you free?

Growing Pains

"Live your life to the fullest!"

We all have heard this saying before, correct? In my opinion, this expression can be very dangerous! Over the years, I've personally witnessed individuals who believe this ideal myth suffer dramatic losses in their lives. The idea of *risking it all for a moment* has its own pros and cons. On one hand, it can be a total blast of utopia. On the other hand, it can be a complete nightmare.

To be very honest with you, we must also prepare ourselves because, in many cases, it leads to us having to say our last goodbyes. I want you to consider that statement (live life to the fullest) as being a game of Russian roulette. The chance of survival is two to one, life or death. There's no other way to explain it.

Definition of *Russian roulette*: "The practice of loading a bullet into one chamber of a revolver (which normally holds six) spinning the cylinder, and then pulling the trigger while pointing the gun at one's own head" (*Oxford Learner's Dictionary*).

Okay. Okay. For the math geniuses out there: Technically, there are six chambers, five of which would be empty. So the chances would be five to one. The viewpoint I am referring to is that you have a fifty-fifty chance, two to one, that that bullet will be in the chamber that is queued up for you.

What is truly worth dying for?

Trying to comprehend this statement would leave a permanent mark on one's subconscious forever. There are too many variables that could be up for debate. Too many scenarios to compare the value of your own life to the saving of something or someone.

Fearless individuals who thrive for consequential fascinations would always leave room for doubt. But still, we anticipate living these fascinations in hopes of gaining deliverance from our own fears. We want to be bullet proof.

I do understand that freewill is a blessing, but what we must admit we have done with it is truly unimaginable. What happened to us? We must stop unintelligently acting like everything is all right. Something is very wrong with our mindsets. Somehow, it's been completely reprogrammed into accepting that problematic mental issues are acceptable.

Challenging Mom

When I was eight years old, I faced another turning point in my life.

For some old reason, my depression of not fitting in led me to my own mental imprisonment. Life was just depression all around, so the habit of thinking deeply about situations embodied my new character. One thought would bother me every time. *What is our purpose in life?*

Striking, isn't it? In my opinion, it is very rare for a kid my age to even be asking himself that kind of question, but like I mentioned earlier, I wasn't any odd ordinary kid. One day, I mustered up the strength to ask my mother this question. With so much grace and warmth in her voice, she would reply, "Son, it's our job to represent God in a manner that brings him glory. His will be done, not ours."

My rebuttal to her response, priceless! "Mom! That's some selfish sh—"

Once I got up from off the floor, I could hear this little echoing voice in my head whisper, *Finish him!*

Terrified the hell out of me. It felt as if God himself wanted me to hear his response to my question. Somehow, at the same time, God had telepathically relayed that same message to my mother. That was my awakening!

Do you remember the game *Mortal Kombat*? There's a character by the name of Scorpion. He wore a yellow-and-black karate uniform with a black mask over his face. He had dark eyes as if he was soulless, and his most epic move was a lethal spear technique move.

His killing blow was announced by an ominous voice commanding, "FINISH HIM!"

A triangle-shaped spearhead attached to chains would come out of his hand. He would thrust it at you, and it would penetrate your virtual torso (body) followed up with a forced upper cut to the face, launching you straight up from off the ground. You're going to love this: his finishing move was the worst. Scorpion would take off his mask and, with fire burning in his eyes, would focus the fury of the flames and launch it straight out his mouth like a flamethrower, burning your entire virtual body. The virtual you was left as a pile of ash.

This is how I had imagined my mother looking at me, like she wanted to do me in with her fiery eyes. That fury was in her eyes. I swore up and down she was the biological mother of Scorpion. He learned those moves from her. Let's just say I got wiser after that encounter. YES, the good old days. Nowadays, you can't even spank your kids to discipline them. It is considered excessive force punishable by imprisonment. In my day, it was called "act right and legally encouraged," generally.

I've grown much since then. Life has given me many lessons in humility. By becoming more aware of how I respond to individual comments and actions, it made me mature significantly. Please do try to live and enjoy your life to the fullest if you're able too. Compare the danger to the thrill. Venture out in the world and see what's in store. If the opportunity arises, take it with thoughtful conscience. The unknown can be scary at times but also a thrill to embark on. If you face your fears today, that absence of fear at that moment can propel you to even further heights in life and help you accomplish your goals.

My only wish for you is to reach for the stars. There is enough room for you to mark your spot. Wish for better days and stop reflecting on those worst days! One thing I've come to grips with: consistency of self-discovering is key to your awakening. You must face ups and downs. The dogma of the human being's experiences is undeniably unavoidable.

Why Is Life So Difficult?

The battle between good and evil will never cease.

In the Book of Genesis, the story of the creation of life gives us a better understanding of the reason why life became so difficult. A celestial law was broken. One rule, one single law, which offered balances to keep us from ever having to suffer trivial trials that would hinder our lives. But instead, we inherited this curse. Yes, a curse!

We were never made to be in rebellion. Our forefather and foremother, Adam and Eve, started it all. Their acts of disobedience toward God created a bloodline (us) of disobedience. Their children are still following in their footsteps. The struggle of doing right gets harder every day with all the distractions of this world. This is why most of us are not awakening and are living as walking zombies. Let's go to the Bible so you can gain clarity.

> Now the serpent was more subtle than any beast of the field which the LORD God had made. And he said unto the woman, "Yea, hath God said, Ye shall not eat of every tree of the garden?"
>
> And the woman said unto the serpent, "We may eat of the fruit of the trees of the garden: But of the fruit of the tree which is in the midst of the garden, God hath said, 'Ye shall not eat of it, neither shall ye touch it, lest ye die.'"
>
> And the serpent said unto the woman, "Ye shall not surely die: For God doth know that in the day ye eat thereof, then your eyes shall be

opened, and ye shall be as gods, knowing good and evil." (Genesis 3:1–6 KJV)

> Now the serpent was more crafty than any other beast of the field that the Lord God had made.
> He said to the woman, "Did God actually say, 'You shall not eat of any tree in the garden'?"
> And the woman said to the serpent, "We may eat of the fruit of the trees in the garden, but God said, 'You shall not eat of the fruit of the tree that is in the midst of the garden, neither shall you touch it, lest you die.'"
> But the serpent said to the woman, "You will not surely die. For God knows that when you eat of it your eyes will be opened, and you will be like God, knowing good and evil." (Genesis 3:1–6 ESV)

If you take time to notice, our culture or language barriers are not the only differences that separate us. For example, have you ever noticed that your presence (energy) is felt differently around those who strive to fit in than of those who would rather stand out? This energy flowing from you goes as far back as the beginning of creation. This is why your intuition is heightened when you begin to mature at a certain age. Your body and mind awaken to different stimulants of your environments. When you come to an understanding of good and evil, you will realize why you become more attracted to light than darkness.

The only reason why our dark side seemed to be more seductive is because it's our immature side. Look at it this way: secrets are hidden in the dark, lying is caused by dark intentions, cheating (dark) thoughts, killing (dark) motives etc. Your light is your intuition, that voice that gets triggered whenever dark toxicity comes your way. This is your soul's (light) natural defense mechanism to surpass any unfamiliar frequencies that would cause you harm.

This is your new transformation! The light might be slow to build up, but it contains swift and deadly power. That's how I felt when I became aware of this new self. Whatever I was becoming, it was going to leave its mark on the world. I knew, eventually, if I could change, I could break this curse from ever corrupting my now new bloodline, my kids.

The mistakes of our past made us this way. When God created you, he gave you a hand that was only meant for you. God needed you to exist in this world. No other can take your place. You were born here on this earth for a reason. God doesn't make mistakes, and you are not one!

We fail to understand this. Perhaps that is the understanding I was searching for. I was seeking purpose.

Critical Thinking, Mustard Seed, and New Gods?

We influence each other more than we know.

If this wasn't true, then the idea of style would never have come into existence. We call it originality; I call it copycats. Human development depends on our understanding, but now we have a multitude of media sites to alter our reality as well as redefine who we truly are simply to impress the masses. Who knew people could make this a full-time job?

Following and acting like Facebook influencers, and thinking you're in the groove by doing so, is just another form of being a copycat. The individuals who think they are showing the world that they can do something potentially dangerous are often showing their ignorance. Followers begin to play Russian roulette. People that follow the shared dangerous activities prove that they do not do their own homework or research or exercise their own critical thinking.

The process of *critical thinking* is being manipulated by professors in college and teachers in the younger ages. We see events influence young minds, and those bright minds get chastised when they try to think on their own and make their own impact on others.

What is *critical thinking*? It is a process of discipline where an individual actively analyzes a concept, gathers information about it, evaluates the pros and cons, observes, reflects, and reasons before forming a belief. For example: You're walking a path down a mountainside, and you come to the edge of a high cliff. You can see the road you need from your vantage point, and it is just below you but a long, long way down with no safe path. You think of the options. You can jump, likely to your death or permanent injury, or you can turn around and find another way down. You are thinking critically, weighing the pros and cons, advantages and disadvantages, the good and the bad outcomes of each choice.

Critical thinking is making an intelligent decision based on facts and abilities. I mention abilities because maybe you are geared up for rappelling down a cliff. There are many factors to consider during a critical-thinking process. Looking at a problem from a different perspective is another factor. My message is simply "Think before you act or respond." This applies to verbal communication as well. Think before you respond.

The human experience is often no longer fun. The computer interaction frenzy has become the new norm in which we have lost complete control. It's our job to teach each other, but what we rely on to do so has become a major problem. We have misused our God-given abilities of thought and truthful communication with attractive fabricating that selfishly lies with unethical truth.

Don't complain about why the world is the way it is when you can do something about it to change it. All it takes is a mustard seed. Plant your seed, and watch it grow. You might be amazed at what you see.

I can see some of the reader's faces reading this, saying, "Who are you to judge?"

I'm not laughing here. I can tell you you're wrong, and I'll tell you why.

See, when you're a kid, much of what I'm saying really doesn't matter to you. Having friends, relationships, toys, video games, etc., these are the things that matter the most. But as you get older, your understanding of life changes. Life comes and goes very quickly. Patience, hard work, and education is required. Let us dive deeper into this concept a mustard seed little bit more.

> Another parable put he forth unto them,
> saying, The kingdom of heaven is like to a grain
> of mustard seed, which a man took, and sowed
> in his field: which indeed is the least of all seeds:

but when it is grown, it is the greatest among
herbs, and becometh a tree, so that the birds of
the air come and lodge in the branches, thereof.
(Matthew 13:31–32 KJV)

He put another parable before them, saying, "The kingdom of heaven is like a grain of
mustard seed that a man took and sowed in his
field. It is the smallest of all seeds but when it
has grown, it is larger than all the garden plants
and becomes a tree so that the birds of the air
come and make nests in its branches." (Matthew
13:31–32 ESV)

Liken the mustard seed to the current influences of today.
One little concept can take over and grow in young minds until it
is a powerful force. Wake up! Use the critical thinking skills of your
thought processing. Look at all sides of the argument. Make your
own decisions and analyze them. Think critically. Do you need to
follow the mustard seed planted by false gods, or do you want to be
your own seed tended by God's love?

Mic check, one, two, one, two. Can you hear me?

Just playing; but seriously, let's see if we can separate the boys
from men, and the women from girls! Let's see if you're still a child
with childish ways or if you have grown up and put away those
childish ways, like the apostle Paul so eloquently put it. You need a
refresher? I got you!

Let's see if you can figure out what is most important in the
world after reading the next verses from the Bible.

When I was a child, I spake as a child, I
understood as a child, I thought as a child but
when I became a man, I put away childish things.

For now we see through a glass, darkly; but
then face to face: now I know in part; but then
shall I know even as also I am known.

And now abideth faith, hope, charity, these three; but the greatest of these is charity. (1 Corinthians 13:11–13 KJV)

When I was a child, I spoke like a child, I thought like a child, I reasoned like a child. When I became a man, I gave up childish ways.

For now we see in a mirror dimly, but then face to face. Now I know in part; then I shall know fully, even as I have been fully known.

So now faith, hope, and love abide, these three; but the greatest of these is love. (1 Corinthians 13:11–13 ESV)

Being a kid at heart is perfectly fine in my opinion, but at the same time, we must be aware of when this behavior is acceptable. Situation does dictate. Pay attention, please, to the energy you put out there in the universe. Our lives are hard enough. Let us try and make a better effort to invest in ourselves. Learn to love yourself. Only then can you truly love one another.

Remember, when you pass away, you will be judged alone. So make your life count while you are still on this earth. Make the right decisions and stop sleeping. Your soul depends on it.

Discussion

- Give an example of how being stylish is just copying someone else.
- Give an example of how people are influenced to change their point of view.
- Can you see how a concept can seem so small and insignificant but grow to influence the many?
- Explain critical thinking, and give an example.
- How will you live life to the fullest?
- Are your thoughts coming from a light place or dark place?

Who Am I?

Now this topic could be debatable, but once again, this is just my opinion.

Ask yourself this. If God revealed to you just who you really were, or are, could you handle this truth? Many have spent most of their lives trying to uncover this puzzling equation, and many have achieved this higher realization of themselves; but unfortunately, many have failed along this journey of consciousness as well.

Educating ourselves is key. Education of self requires excessive patience, and self-control on our part when trying to align ourselves with the divine (God), but by doing so, it is possible to accomplish. If done successfully, you will open gates within yourself that contain enormous strength, clarity, and power that will change you forever. In fact, it may even scare you on what you unlock about yourself. Along your journey, you will bump into many walls, obstacles that may, at first, seem impossible to conquer; but you were built strong enough to handle it, which makes it so beautiful.

Tears of joy will flow like rivers down your face, and an unbelievable relief of stress will overwhelm you as you process the idea that you are now free. Free from the chains that caged you with unrealistic beliefs that were taught to you your entire life. History has proven this countless times. That's why it's very important that you protect your energy from any toxic behaviors that may prevent you from gaining this precious gift.

Many have fallen and risen and fallen again but still got back up to continue their pursuit of making their dreams come true. Somewhere in that journey was a reality check. A never-ending journey but worth every bit of it. When you begin to understand that you are now eating from the table that God has prepared for you in the presence of your enemies (Psalm 23:5), you will come to terms accepting the fact that these individuals were never your enemies. In fact, they were hidden opportunists serving the lessons you needed to propel you to greatness.

Let me share with you a comforting verse. Well, it is a well-known psalm. Psalm means "a sacred song or hymn."

> The Lord is my shepherd; I shall not want.
> He maketh me to lid down in green pastures; he leadeth me beside the still waters.
> He restoreth my soul: he leadeth me in the paths of righteousness for his name's sake.
> Yea, though I walk through the valley of the shadow of death, I will fear no evil: for thou art with me; thy rod and thy staff they comfort me.
> Thou preparest a table before me in the presence of mine enemies: thou anointest my head with oil; my cup runneth over.
> Surely goodness and mercy shall follow me all the days of my life: and I will dwell in the house of the Lord for ever. (Psalm 23 KJV)

> The Lord is my shepherd; I shall not want.
> He makes me lie down in green pastures.
> He leads me beside still waters.
> He restores my soul.
> He leads me in the paths of righteousness
> for his name's sake.
> Even though I walk through the valley of
> the shadow of death,
> I will fear no evil,
> For you are with me;
> your rod and your staff,
> they comfort me.

You prepare a table before me
in the presence of my enemies;
you anoint my head with oil;
my cup overflows.
Surely goodness and mercy shall follow me
all the days of my life,
and I shall dwell in the house of the Lord
Forever. (Psalm 23 ESV)

Such a calming, comforting verse, don't you think? Peace and reassurance of self is all we really need and desire in this life. Everything else, in my opinion, is considered a bonus. If we're never meant to be understood, we were meant to stick out. Read the Psalm again and breathe. Clear your mind and consider this. You ask "Who am I?" when your time might be better spent pondering the question "Who do I want to be?"

Reality Check

The absence of light is darkness, correct?

Well, you are that light that is supposed to eradicate the dark. So rest assured, we must shine. If you haven't figured that out already, I do have a story that backs up my statements.

True story. This was my reality check. One of many to follow.

When my first son was born, a mixture of emotions overwhelmed me. Feelings of happiness, indignation, fulfillment, despair, and utter rage happened all at once. My heart felt completely torn apart. The thought of knowing I had to now care for a child completely altered my plans for everything I had planned for my life. Yes! I was selfish as hell.

Okay, ladies, calm down. I'll say it for you. "If you can lay down and make it, you're sure as hell going to raise it!" Happy now? I totally agree with all of you! The dilemma, honestly, wasn't about having a child: it was the patronizing overwhelming feeling of not knowing *how* to raise a child.

Remember what I mentioned earlier? I wasn't raised by my father, so having to emulate a father figure to a child was completely above my understanding. My life wasn't surrounded by loving male role models. Instead, just men with narcissistic mindsets and dominating, brute, savage behaviors represented the role.

So as I held my son for the very first time, all I could do was stare at him and mumble under my breath. "What in the hell am I supposed to do with this thing?"

Completely neglecting the fact that he was a human being, I spoke of him as if he was some kind of unwanted trash resting in my hand, something that needed to be disposed of quickly. Apparently, one of the male nurses passing by heard me. He had such a huge smile on his face as he approached, so relieved the procedure went as planned, but that smile completely changed immediately into a frown. His rebuttal to my statement? "How about you be a father and raise him!"

As he looked back at me, the glare in his eyes was full of intense fire. I knew I was in the wrong. Undeniably. What was I thinking about, saying those words? I asked myself if I had disrespected him and every proud father out there in the world who had a boy for their first child. It's a father's dream still today to have their first child a boy. Here I was, in the presence of this man, being so ungrateful and undeserving. Embarrassment and hurt, all at the same time, hit my heart. All I could do was put my head down in shame.

The embarrassment didn't end there. My son heard my voice and opened his eyes for the very first time. If a stare could kill, he had it. He stared directly into my eyes with his pitch-dark eyes filled with great fury, not empathetic to my feelings at all. It was as if he was telepathically telling me how disappointed he was in me and in hearing the words I just spoke. See, the eyes are a mirror to our soul, and what his soul relayed to me was, "I didn't ask to be here! But now that I'm here alive, you better look after me."

From that moment on, the walls around my heart and mind completely shattered. It felt as if all my past hurts, regrets, and disap-pointments were now gone. Considering the effect of what just his stare had done to me, at that very moment I just wanted to say to my son, "Thank you! You just saved me from going straight to hell for those words." Do you see what I meant about the hidden potential in us? It doesn't matter what age you are; you just don't know who you may encounter that could change who you are. Just because you haven't seen their potential doesn't mean they don't have it.

Never underestimate the power of the human spirit!

God had given me a chance to right the wrongs my father had made with me. I never felt real love from my father, so here was God giving me the chance to break that cursed cycle of hate with me and my son.

Now I was able to show my son the love he deserved. I was aware I could break this curse from ever repeating again by doing right by my own son now. Obligated to provide protection, love, and overall guidance, it humbled me. By grace we are saved (Ephesians 2:8), and by God's love we are saved.

> For by grace are ye saved through faith; and that not of yourselves; it is the gift of God. (Ephesians 2:8 KJV)

> For by grace you have been saved through faith. And this is not your own doing; it is the gift of God. (Ephesians 2:8 ESV)

That night, I dedicated his spirit back to God as a gift from me. In that very moment, I felt as if the room was crowded by many guardian angels and archangels posted alongside us, giving a circle of protection for us both. A dedication ceremony was occurring, and the angels were the hosts. I'd like to share some definitions and revelations that I had.

Definition of *dedication ceremonies*: "A ceremony to mark the official completion or opening of something" (*Merriam-Webster's Collegiate Dictionary*).

Biblical definition of *dedication ceremonies*: "a general term used in the Bible to describe an act of setting apart or consecrating persons or things to God (or gods), person, sacred work, or ends. The act is usually accompanied by an announcement of what is being done or intended and by prayer asking for divine approval and blessing" (StudyLight.org/dictionaries).

Then, from out of nowhere, these words came out of my mouth.

"Dear heavenly Father, please, I beg of thee, grant me the strength in this hour. I cannot do this alone, my God! I need your help. For I am a broken man who has suffered much from guilt and pain which still consume my heart. Help me become a better man so I may raise him right. According to your will, and not my own. I dedicate his soul back to you, my Lord. Do with it as you wish. Make him strong enough to survive this life. Cover him with the blood of your son Lord Jesus Christ. Grant him the wisdom and understanding and the strength needed to endure this life. Shine your light on him so he may know it was you who saved him this night. In Jesus Christ's name, I pray. Amen."

At that moment, my son reopened his eyes. A glow came into his eyes so bright it was as if it was the burning sun itself, overshadowing the darkness that was once seen in his eyes. He then gave me a little smile then yawned as he fell back to sleep in my arms. Thanks, son (Bryson Emmanuel Young). You saved my life and my soul from facing damnation! To your mother, Andressa Young, thank you for having him and putting up with all my sh——t. True story.

No matter what life throws at you, always remember who puts up with you. Remember, they, too, suffer much hurt and pain dealing with you. Never forget, no matter what. Have respect for all mothers, no matter what. It's ordered by God to not only respect the mothers but the fathers as well. This is the fifth commandment. That is very important, so don't neglect it.

> Honour thy father and thy mother: that thy
> days may be long upon the land which the LORD
> thy God giveth thee. (Exodus 20:12 KJV)

> Honor your father and your mother, that
> your days may be long in the land that the LORD
> your God is giving you. (Exodus 20:12 ESV)

All that is hidden in the dark shall come into light. You can deceive people all you like, but you won't deceive God. Believe in him or not, your heart and soul will be judged one day. You will pay for your transgressions made here on earth.

You know what is deemed to be very interesting? It is commonly accepted, the idea that there is a devil, but so many can't accept the fact that there is a God. Someone please tell me: if that is the case, then who created your soul? The soul that the devil is always chasing after, trying to collect.

Don't worry, I'll wait… Exactly!

Before we move on to roadblocks that might be placed in your path to a new beginning, let's touch back to the copycat syndrome. I understand the fear of missing out. This includes the fear of not fitting in to the secular world. This is also known by the acronym FOMO (Fear of Missing Out). Don't worry. Once you have overcome the obstacles ahead, others might just have a FOMO on what you have discovered!

Change your mindset people. It amazes me sometimes that what we believe to be reality really isn't. We seem to always get surprised when life reveals the truth to us. In our society today, we have adapted to that very dangerous behavior called mimicry.

Definition of *mimicry*: "the action or art of imitating someone or something, typically in order to entertain or ridicule" (*Oxford Learner's Dictionary*).

History has shown us that the past does repeat itself. We were doomed from the beginning to make the same mistakes our predecessors made. We go to church praying to God, asking for forgiveness of our sins, then repeat those same sins all over again. I'm guilty of this as well. When the wheel of life spins and it's your time to change, be ready. I'm warning you first. Keep cutting corners like everyone else and the grave digger will be the only one who will remember your name!

Discussion

- Reflect on the following phrases. Apply it to where you are now and how it will affect where you want to be.

  Consistency is the key.

  Education is the key.

  Cutting corners. (Think of examples of where you might have cut a corner to get to a goal. How did it turn out? Could it have been better if you followed the rules/ guidelines?)

  Having a life-changing event. (Decide what a life-changing event is to you.)

- Have you invested in the wrong type of education just to fit into society?
- Do you have any regrets not investing in yourself as much as you invested in others?
- Do you regret depending on others in order to succeed in life.
- What is codependency?
- What events occurred in your life which took you off your path?
- How often did you neglect yourself to please others?

Fear

In this part of the book, I must warn you all that things will get very intense.

Many have done intensive studies on the subject of fear and brought a great deal of light on the consequences that come along with it. However, there are many who still deviate from calling it what it really is. My responsibility to you and everyone who comes across this book is to take it a little further. With that being said, I will not take the same route as the others have.

This is not a game to me! Forget researching. Forget fabricating ideas just to make the subject fascinating. Forget elaborating key ideas just to sound educated. This is the harsh truth. I'm bringing you straight into the battlefield, reader, so strap on your guns and gear. Check your boot laces and make sure they are tight. We're going in!

This includes our elders. Listen up if you would, please. Speaking and working with our elders, I have observed and learned a little about feelings, expressed or not. Elders have the fear of no longer having purpose. We can note them clashing with young people, either gently or not so gently. Elders have other problems to which the youth cannot relate to.

They, too, have regrets, and some elders will take those secrets to the grave with them. Keep in mind that the journey I am taking you on does not end in your younger ages but continues through elderhood and to the death of the body. We all have fears. It manifests differently in everyone.

Fear has destroyed and continues to destroy the hopes and dreams of many lives still to this day, driving many to madness and others to killing themselves just to try to run away from it. You must understand that your past, present, and future all play a deadly role in why fears exist. Why? Because the demonic spirit of fear will never die if it is allowed to continue to exist in your life. No matter where you live or where you run to, it will follow you until the end of time.

Fear lives in the shadows as well as in the light, and no one ever talked about that. What does this remind you of? Correct: the devil himself. It moves around and within everyone without asking for permission to invade your life. We all keep dark secrets, correct? Some people know of them; others just pray it never gets exposed. The truth is, as crazy as it may sound, our very existence depends on it!

Without fear, you will not recognize an obstacle. Life is a labyrinthic design. Finding, or losing, your way through the labyrinth can lead to discovering your own fear or bravery, or even finding true love. It might even help someone realize wealth and power. Fear can reveal your biggest obstacle. That block that keeps you from moving forward in life. With just a small fragment of your imagination, it can turn a peaceful memory into your worst nightmare.

Thoughts of why you haven't gotten further in life will always arise. Excuses you once made will no longer work, and the disbelief of why certain decisions had to be made are all part of fear. Have you ever, in your life, been so paralyzed by something or someone you feared that you couldn't even think? Were you unable to move on because the uncertainties haunted you? Ghosts of constant battles of negative behaviors and selfish ideas will hunt you down, and the worst of them all, denial (another demon).

Give yourself time to reflect on what I just mentioned and tell me if I am wrong. Many have spent years just trying to overcome it, but in the end, all that was lost was their peace. Here are three really important questions we all must ask ourselves. Think about them. I've left space for you to write your own reflections.

1. Why does it take being afraid to force us to be brave?
2. Is it necessary to be afraid when trying to move forward?
3. Do our faith and beliefs revolve around being afraid?

Over time and after constant failure and lack of self-discipline, life seems to always overwhelm us. Then what happens next? We find safety in isolating ourselves from everyone and everything. Fear creeps into our lives like a thief in the night. It's as if we are constantly being surrounded by mischievous demonic spirits, whispering to us in our ears, "You're going to fail," "Stop trying," "You're going to die here," and "It wasn't your fault!"

This devil feeds on your doubts and latches onto you like a bloodsucking leech. The more you try to break free from it, the more it drains your blood and grows until its belly is full. By then it's too late, and all you can do is pray and hope God will help you through it.

Why is all of this happening to me right now?

This is another very important question you will find yourself asking. You have, haven't you? The answer is simple. Fear is leading you to that condition we call the awakening state which can be a rude realization of disagreeable facts or a renewal of interest in something. Upon awakening, fear might be your first response.

Definition of *awaking*: "an act of waking from sleep; an act or moment of becoming suddenly aware of something; a rude awakening to the disagreeable facts, a renewal of interest in religion, especially in a community; a revival."

Awakening may happen when your thoughts begin to run wild while all the traumas you faced in your life seem to develop a life of their own. Fear of anything and nothing might grow in those immediate thoughts of awakening. These traumas can cause many to be driven into madness and even develop suicidal thoughts. You begin to develop extremely bad habits that you assume are necessary in order to help you cope with everything. Pay close attention when you're in this state of mind. It will lead you to severe depression.

Intense pain and massive blockages of your own emotions will occur, and seeking help will seem like an embarrassment because your ego and pride are now suffering. Your darkest fears are trying to manifest themselves into your reality. You must gain control of your emotions. Understand something: You will have no other choice but to face this quasi-evil spirit called fear. You cannot move forward in life until you do.

Never ever tell yourself it's too late to face your fears. Consider this to be the ultimate weapon chosen by life: a weapon forged from the fires of others who have lived and died, leaving nothing but a trail mark of their blood, sweat, and tears as evidence that they too had to face this immortal spirit. If only this truth was made available beforehand, maybe they would've still been here; instead, all we have are the books written about them.

I don't know about you, but I would've preferred them to be alive to tell their own story through their own mouths of how they made it through their battles instead of reading. In life, word of mouth carries so much weight. Too much information can overwhelm you, especially when you're confused already. Some may even say that too much information can alter your entire reality of what we perceive as truth.

You know what really made me take this time and effort to really present this chapter to you? It was a chapter I read in a psalm of the Holy Bible. This made everything clear to me about why fear is misunderstood by many. This spirit can be so heavy it will bring you to your knees and make you want to cry. Having this spirit come within you can hurt your very soul.

Look at what happened to our Lord and Savior in the following verses. It's long, I know, but it's so very important to see his point of view as he died. I will only use the English Standard Version here to save time and space.

> My God, my God, why have you forsaken
> me? Why are you so far from saving me, from the
> words of my groaning?

O my God, I dry by day, but you do not answer, and by night, but I find no rest.

Yet you are holy, enthroned on the praises of Israel.

In you our fathers trusted; they trusted, and you delivered them.

To you they cried and were rescued; in you they trusted and were not put to shame.

But I am a worm and not a man, scorned by mankind and despised by the people. (Psalm 22:1–31 ESV)

One night, to further my understanding of this spiritual walk I've been on, I decided to lay down and stare at the ceiling, once again praying, asking God, "Why is fear so important?"

I know, a very strange question, you presume. But in my opinion, it was a true, genuine question. Have you ever pondered this question before? When an individual is exposed to some type of fear, there's an energetic shift that occurs. It's a feeling so great that it literally paralyzes you to your core. The emotion alone can suffocate you, causing extreme panic attacks.

Stages of fear: paralysis, inefficiency, catastrophizing, holding on, self-doubt, normalcy, and disbelief" (Arthur Miller, 1953).

Memories are also formed as a result of fear. Some good; some not. Your body has a physical reaction to fear that manifests differently for us all. This is there; the fight-or-flight response comes in. You can respond in fighting mode or run away. Some people even become paralyzed in place. Some cry. Some scream. Our response determines how we move on. And we can learn to adjust our response.

An acronym associated with *fear*: False Evidence Appearing Real. Of course, we know that the evidence is not always false. It can be very real, and fear is a very legitimate response to keep us safe. But there is an abundance of evidence that is fearful only because of evidence we have placed in our minds—or that others have wormed into our minds—that might not be true.

So like all things that ever happened in my life, something had to break for me to receive a revelation of clarity. What was I afraid of? Tears started to run down my face, and all I could do was close my eyes, shaking my head and wondering why. Then at that very moment, a thought popped up in my head, and I could remember my mother saying, "Son, don't be scared. God will answer your prayers. Go read Psalm 91."

It's funny, but the older you get, the more you remember things that never meant much to you when you were younger. Remember earlier when I talked about what was important to us when we were young? This time I decided to listen. I reached for the Bible and found the scripture.

> He that dwelleth in the secret place of the most High shall abide under the shadow of the Almighty.
>
> I will say of the LORD, He is my refuge and my fortress: my God; in him will I trust.
>
> Surely he shall deliver thee from the snare of the fowler, and from the noisome pestilence.
>
> He shall cover thee with his feathers, and under his wings shalt thou trust: his truth shall be thy shield and buckler.
>
> Thou shalt not be afraid for the terror by night; nor for the arrow that flieth by day;
>
> Nor for the pestilence that walketh in darkness; nor for the destruction that wasteth at noonday.
>
> A thousand shall fall at thy side, and ten thousand at thy right hand; but it shall not come nigh thee.
>
> Only with thine eyes shalt thou behold and see the reward of the wicked. Because thou hast made the LORD, which is my refuge, even the most High, thy habitation;

There shall no evil befall thee, neither shall any plague come nigh thy dwelling.

For he shall give his angels charge over thee, to keep thee in all thy ways.

They shall bear thee up in their hands, lest thou dash thy foot against a stone.

Thou shalt tread upon the lion and adder: the young lion and the dragon shalt thou trample under feet.

Because he hath set his love upon me, therefore will I deliver him: I will set him on high, because he hath known my name.

He shall call upon me, and I will answer him: I will be with him in trouble; I will deliver him, and honour him.

With long life will I satisfy him, and shew him my salvation. (Psalm 91 KJV)

He who dwells in the shelter of the Most High will abide in the shadow of the Almighty.

I will say to the Lord, "My refuge and my fortress, my God, in whom I trust."

For he will deliver you from the snare of the fowler and from the deadly pestilence.

He will cover you with his pinions, and under his wings you will find refuge; his faithfulness is a shield and buckler.

You will not fear the terror of the night, nor the arrow that flies by day,

nor the pestilence that stalks in darkness, nor the destruction that wastes at noonday.

A thousand may fall at your side, ten thousand at your right hand, but it will not come near you.

You will only look with your eyes and see the recompense of the wicked.

Because you have made the Lord your dwelling place—the Most High, who is my refuge[b]—

no evil shall be allowed to befall you, no plague come near your tent.

For he will command his angels concerning you to guard you in all your ways.

On their hands they will bear you up, lest you strike your foot against a stone.

You will tread on the lion and the adder; the young lion and the serpent you will trample underfoot.

"Because he holds fast to me in love, I will deliver him; I will protect him, because he knows my name.

When he calls to me, I will answer him; I will be with him in trouble; I will rescue him and honor him.

With long life I will satisfy him and show him my salvation." (Psalm 91 ESV)

Psalm 91 is basically saying that if you dwell in the house of the Lord, you will have God's protection. This does not mean that no accident or illness will ever injure or kill you. God's rescue might be what you want. He will recover you, and that just might mean taking your home with him. That could be a fear-filled consideration as well but one that leads to peace.

You know, fear has been a never-ending battle in which many lives and homes have been destroyed. So much so, for me, that there were times when waking up in the mornings was no longer a joy. We are suffering because of lack of knowledge of how to deal with it. It is causing many to lose faith in God. It separates families, relationships, and perpetrates the idea that we can't even love ourselves. Speaking about this scares people into believing there's no hope!

This is our ultimate test! Will you allow your fears to stop you from becoming free, or will you allow it to stop you while this lingering question remains: "Am I too weak to survive this?"

This world we all live in is influenced by both dark and light energies, and both scare us. This is why learning about self-love is very important to me. Without wisdom and educating ourselves to gain a different perspective on who and why we are the way we are, we will continue to be lost with no hope of being found. Remember, it's your choice if you allow your fears to stop you; but if you have a dream worth fighting for, this battle will make you stronger and more powerful than you ever thought you could ever become.

No one had ever taught me this, take it from me. I had to witness and learn this from all the carnage that was left behind in the aftermath. These are some other questions that helped me realize the damage that was done to me. Maybe it will help you along your journey fighting the devilish spirits of fear and denial.

Ask yourself the following questions then ask yourself why it happened.

1. Have I ever allowed my fears to stop me from achieving my dreams?
2. Have I ever allowed anyone to continue deceiving me when I knew the truth all along?
3. Have I ever pushed away the individuals who really believed in me because I didn't believe in myself?
4. Have I ever stopped myself from believing that real love still exists just because I've been hurt so many times in the past?
5. Have I ever placed my wants before my needs? (Understand there is a difference we will discuss in a later chapter.)
6. Could I have been much stronger in defending myself instead of giving in to someone or something that wasn't for my highest good?
7. Have I ever allowed my thoughts to deceive me into believing I wasn't good enough? (Think of what you had to sacrifice.)

8.   Have I ever lost faith in God's promise to me where he said, "I will never leave or forsake you"?

9.   Have I ever been inpatient in situations that I felt wouldn't work out for me due to my lack of faith?

10. Have I ever lost my way because of my spiritual practices or lack thereof?

11. Have I ever allowed my past failures to dictate my future?

12. Have I ever allowed other people's opinions to control and influence me into walking the wrong path that wasn't for me?

13. Why don't I believe and trust in myself enough to succeed?

I know that was a lot of questions, but there is so much to learn about how fear interweaves itself in our bodies and minds; whole studies have been conducted on its effects on ourselves and others. It is something that we all need to investigate on how it affects our own lives.

Analyzing yourself is a very tedious process. There is a practice called shadow work.

If you do the shadow work on yourself, you will find out the real reason why you keep repeating these harsh cycles in your life. Learn how to liberate your own soul from domination.

Definition of *shadow work*: "working with your unconscious mind to uncover the parts of yourself that you repress and hide from yourself. This can include traumas or part of your personality that you subconsciously consider undesirable" (*Oxford Learner's Dictionary*).

Definition of *domination*: "the exercise of control or influence over someone or something, or the state of being controlled" (*Oxford Learner's Dictionary*).

Practice this skill of shadow work please. By doing so, you will understand the root of all your problems. Ask any therapist about what I'm saying. If you ask yourself the right questions, you will find that you already know the truth.

Believing in yourself is a test. Doubting yourself is a process. It takes more time to find the truth than to come up with a lie disguising the truth. Fear is necessary at times, especially when you're doubting yourself; it checks the angry spirit. I do believe Cicely Tyson once quoted that in the movie *Hoodlum*: "It's good to be afraid sometimes. It checks the angered spirit." Great movie. I believe that was the exact quote.

Scientific studies have shown that when a person becomes fearful, blood rushes to the brain, causing the neural circuitry system to become unbalanced. Basically, we begin to not think straight. Our behavior switches in ways that become uncontrollable. Our emotions go haywire, and our responses slow down.

In Harvard University, a group of students studied the neurons that travel up and down our spine, which trigger our responses. Through intensive research, they found out that the moment we become fearful, the nervous system sends signals that would have travelled fifty times up and down our spine before the body even got the chance to respond. Amazing. In other words, our body would have gone into shutdown mode, causing a delay in response. Our brain won't respond correctly.

It comes to a point in our lives when we will have to say, "Enough is enough!" Our greatest strength is self-control. Facing our fears is one way of learning this. So please, love yourself enough to never give up. And fight back. Do it for your kids. Do it for the ones you love. Do it for yourself. Don't let your fears steal your glory. I believe in you, so believe in yourself!

Maya Angelou (American memoirist, poet, and Civil Rights activist) once said:

> What is a fear of living? It's being preeminently afraid of dying. It is not doing what you came here to do, out of timidity and spinelessness. The antidote is to take full responsibility for yourself—for the time you take up and the space you occupy. If you don't know what you're here to do, then just do some good.

Curiosity

For many years now, I've debated with myself on whether or not the Scriptures were true based on the idea that we could find paradise right here on earth.

Don't misunderstand me now. We can experience great moments, but to insist we can experience paradise, in my opinion, that's a little paradoxical to believe. There are too many variables to consider. In my opinion, I'm unsure that this is accurate because we spend too much time projecting our insecurities onto one another.

It's troublesome to me to be a witness of all the pain going on throughout the world with the lack of consideration for one another, hatred, and lack of loyalty. Who in their right mind would believe this idea of a magnificent dream of utopia could be true? When I was around nine years old, the very first book I became interested in was the Holy Bible. For as far back as I could remember, the Book of Revelation was always thrown in my face. Whenever I would ask the adults a question, everyone would direct me to the Bible.

What a mystery of life I was already living! Everyone spoke of this book so highly it began to seem more relevant to me that it held the answers to why things are the way they are. So many people at church would discuss this book. Obsessed and completely fed up with so many opinions on what was in it, I finally decided to find out why. I knew I was too young, but I still tried to read this book on my own. I failed horribly at it initially. Yet for some odd reason, I was beginning to gain a weird sense of understanding of it. Verse by verse, I just kept breaking the words down until I comprehended what it was saying.

Have you ever been so angry and frustrated at something you just grew the urge to fight? I was so pugnacious I would throw the Bible as hard as I could on the ground and walk away. The writing style of the language was unfamiliar to me. Most of the words I couldn't even say; but as you may have already come to be aware about me, it was weird. It fit my character very well indeed.

Something alluring inside the Bible kept pulling me back to that book. It became very clear to me that I was on the right track. Every time I read the Word, I felt as if I was being sucked into a portal straight into an unknown world that felt as if I lived and experienced it before. Many nights, after reading, I would find myself falling asleep right on the pages. Many times, I would wake up feeling drained and depleted of energy, as if I had an out-of-body experience. Knowing this alone scared the living daylights out of me. Yet still I felt compelled to continue reading.

The stories were fascinating and very dark to me. Filled with uncharted depth and twists, it felt as if it was a scary story written by Stephen King himself. I love his books, but that's beside the point. I felt privileged and honored in reading this book, the Book of Revelation. Having no one to tell me to stop made it even better. In fact, the idea that someone decided to create such a story bothered me to the point it made me ask another question. "How is it possible that the individuals who had done these awful deeds lived to talk about it and weren't locked up?"

Now you may be wondering to yourself, "Why in the world is a nine-year-old boy even reading something as complex as this, the Truth?" I have no clue, honestly, but one thing was for certain: God doesn't make any mistakes! I knew there was a reason behind my curiosity.

Pain

Let's take a pause and think about this curious question for just a moment before we continue to go even further into another curious obstacle. "How deep are you?"

Earlier I showed you that I was deep in my spirituality, but it was not always so. I was deep into some other stuff but crawled and fought my way out. So how deep are you in either one direction or the other? How much of what kind of pain have you been buried in? How far down the rabbit hole are you? What is your smile hiding?

Understanding pain and suffering is part of life, and many still don't understand why. This is not a topic that should be taken lightly, but it is necessary. *Enduring or surviving painful situations develops character*. This includes mental and emotional pain and suffering that must be processed through an already-confused mind. Agreed? It reveals the hidden secrets about who you really are.

There is a process, an inner struggle you must face and master in order for you to maintain control over yourself and your emotions. It is a tug-of-war between your own light and darkness within. One minute, you can feel valuable; the next, very disquieted. Life will hit you so hard at times you will pray for death and hope it doesn't come. Everything that has happened to us has made us who we are today. The trick is finding the origin of that triggering pain and dealing with it.

Escaping this harsh reality is what many of us tend to always think about, yet we still find ourselves having to deal with it. Killing yourself is an easy way out. Simply not worth it in my opinion, no matter what you are going through. Trust me, I will not say to you I haven't felt that way. In fact, I even tried a few times, but God! That's all I have to say about that.

We all cry alone because of unresolved past trauma. We drink and do drugs in hopes to wipe away the sorrows we face. At times it seems to work, but in all actuality, all it does is keep us in despair and on the road to a darker nightmare. You see, when you lose yourself, nothing matters anymore. Not your kids, family, lovers, spouse, or even God. Everything seems to be stripped away from your heart, and all that's left is an empty vessel to be used by the devil. I know that feeling all too well. It cost me my kids, my marriage, my faith, my hope, and my dreams.

Every night I would think of ways to destroy myself because I felt cursed. Used and betrayed by those who claimed to love me, forgotten by friends who claimed to have my back, broken and unsatisfied with my life, the devil became a good friend to me. I had no desire to love anyone anymore. Sex with a woman felt more like an unwaning burden simply because I felt nothing inside anymore. I felt I just wanted to simply walk my path alone and not be bothered by anyone. All I could think about was murder, to lash out in pain at anyone who would smile in my face simply because they spoke of their life being so great.

My heart became cold. My eyes changed. That new spirit that God gave to me? I prayed for him to take it back. Let me rot like every decayed body in the ground, or I promised to take whoever hurt me with me to the grave. This is how I felt after suffering so much pain. I felt cursed. Life, to me, wasn't the same. I was a product of the people, and this world hated me, so I hated the world in the same way. I've changed since then. I'd be a hypocrite if I didn't admit that I'd never felt pain on a level that would have made anyone go insane.

Just a random but poignant thought: "Do you believe the real reason why we all experience pain here on earth is connected to the suffering our Lord Jesus Christ had to go through?"

He was scorned and beaten by man. Brutally assaulted, chastised, betrayed, and killed just to save us from death. Isn't that what is happening to us now today? We betray one another, forsake our kids, and brutally mishandle our children and women, just entertaining these crowds of devilish vultures who prey on our weaknesses. We cheer for mayhem behind closed doors then want to speak and do something to stop it only when it comes to our own front doors. Interesting, don't you think?

Let's go deeper.

There was a man by the name Jorge Agustin Nicolás Ruiz de Santayana y Borrás, also known as George Santayana. No. Not Santana. George Santayana was a philosopher, poet, and novelist in the early 1800s. He was regarded as one of the greatest educators of his time. His understanding of history, and his unique style, led to the idea that spirit and nature played a huge part in the reconciliation of us. His most famous quote, if not the best quote ever, relates to everything that's being discussed here: "Those who cannot remember the past are condemned to repeat."

Who in God's green earth gave him this revelation? How did he come to terms with understanding this truth? What did he mean by this? You will receive another poignant example of the meaning of Mr. Santayana's statement later in this chapter.

This made me think extremely hard about my life and this life. Adam and Eve were the first human flesh created on earth. They were also the first to disobey God's law.

Moving forward, to the time our God tries to help us again when he sends us his Son, our Lord Jesus Christ, who is also known as God in the flesh. We disobeyed and betrayed him again. Now here is a sacred book, discussing the return of Jesus Christ (God), and we are already on the verge of repeating the same actions again. Don't you agree this is strange? Or is it prophetic? Mr. Santayana was correct. We are repeating this cycle again.

In my opinion, pain is necessary, as are the struggles that come with it. God is up to something, but what could that be?

> For my thoughts are not your thoughts, neither are your ways my ways, saith the Lord.
> For as the heavens are higher than the earth, so are my ways higher than your ways, and my thoughts than your thoughts. (Isaiah 55:8–9 KJV)

> For my thoughts are not your thoughts, neither are your ways my ways, declares the Lord.
> For as the heavens are higher than the earth, so are my ways higher than your ways and my thoughts than your thoughts. (Isaiah 55:8–9 ESV)

Sometimes, I wish the Lord would just speak plain English and tell us the answers. Have you ever felt that way? Who am I to question the Lord? But wait, are we not his sons and daughters? Are we not his children? Then we have every right to question our Father. If he already knows everything, then it shouldn't surprise him then. Right or wrong? At this point in my life, I'm going to God about everything. Society's brainwashing methods of control is now wearing off. Pain may lead us to our deaths, but at least we can die with some truths.

Over the years I've learned we are our own *blessing blockers*. What I mean is, we are the only ones who can stop our blessing from ever reaching us. Religion is a scapegoat to share our opinions, and religion can be confusing. The only difference is, we use the experience we gain from churches to justify religious facts, while the others use studies from books to justify secular facts. As a result, it creates total confusion amongst us, and killing each other seems to be the only result to solving everything, even our religious beliefs.

This nation was founded by blood, and it, too, shall die in blood! Agree with me or not, but one day, this will all end. No money or powerful army will be able to stop it from happening. We can all agree on this, correct?

> Faith is not a gift! It's something that must be earned. (My quote—don't you dare take it.)

Without enduring pain, we won't understand life. But there is a promise.

> Blessed is the man that endureth temptation: for when he is tried, he shall receive the crown of life, which the Lord hath promised to them that love him. (James 1:12 KJV)

> Blessed is the man who remains steadfast under trial, for when he has stood the test he will receive the crown of life, which God has promised to those who love him. (James 1:12 ESV)

Keep this promise in mind if you don't remember anything else. Always keep your head up and know this: You're not alone in this fight! This is not a normal battle we all face today. This is a battle between good and evil, light versus darkness. Whichever side you choose, one thing is for certain: you will have to go through pain. Time is running out, so choose wisely.

The following section is that other example of people repeating history today in their everyday lives. Think of this as a little history lesson.

There was a man by the name of *Willie Lynch*. Remember this name and look it up if you have to.

Our country developed from his system. Willie Lynch, a British slave owner from the West Indies in the early 1700s, developed a foolproof method on how to control black slaves. Many scholars would agree to disagree that Mr. Lynch's method derived from an Anglo-Saxon's idea—a method that ensured a master-slave relationship as a way of dominance and control.

Still to this day, there are debates if the speech was just a hoax or if it was another method to spark the already-growing fire of the racial tension, which was already occurring in the United States. Mr. Lynch's system was not only flawless but it would also guarantee to repeat every generation. Here is what was said: "It doesn't matter on the color of an individual. The system itself will work on everyone, period." This is not the whole speech but the part you must be aware of.

> Gentlemen: I greet you here on the bank of the James River in the year of our lord, one thousand seven hundred and twelve. First, I shall thank you, the gentlemen of the colony of Virginia, for bringing me here. I am here to help you solve some of your problems with slaves. Your invitation reached me in my modest plantation in the West Indies where I have experimented with some of the newest and still the oldest method for control of slaves. Ancient Rome would envy us if my program is implemented. As our boat sailed south on the James River, named for our illustrious KING JAMES, whose BIBLE we CHERISH, I saw enough to know that our problem is not unique. While Rome used cords of wood as crosses for standing human bodies along the old highways in great numbers, you are here using the tree and the rope on occasion.

Now brace yourself, here comes the boom:

In my bag, I have a fool proof method for controlling your slaves. I guarantee every one of you that if installed it will control the slaves for at least three hundred years. My method is simple, any member of your family or any OVERSEER can use it. I have outlined a number of differences among the slaves, and I take these differences and make them bigger. I use FEAR, DISTRUST, and ENVY for control purposes. These methods have worked on my modest plantation in the West Indies, and it will work throughout the SOUTH. Take this simple little list of differences and think about them. On the top of my list is *age*, but it is only there because it starts with an A. The second is *color* or shade. There is INTELLIGENCE, SIZE, SEX, SIZE OF PLANTATION, ATTITUDE of owner, whether the slaves live in the valley, on a hill, east or west, north, south, have fine or coarse hair, or is tall or short. Now that you have a list of differences, I shall give you an outline of action. But before that, I shall assure you that DISTRUST IS STRONGER THAN TRUST, AND ENVY IS STRONGER THAN ADULATION, RESPECT, OR ADMIRATION.

The Black slave, after receiving this indoctrination, shall carry on and will become self-refueling and self-generating for hundreds of years, maybe thousands. Don't forget you must pitch the old Black men versus the young Black males, and the young Black male against the old Black male. You must use the dark-skinned slaves versus the light-skinned slaves. You must use the female versus the male, and the male versus the female. You must always have your servants and overseers distrust all Blacks, but it is necessary that your

slaves trust and depend on us. Gentlemen, these
kits are your keys to control, use them. Never
miss an opportunity. My plan is guaranteed, and
the good thing about this plan is that if used
intensely for one year the slave will remain per-
petually distrustful.

How crazy is that? Now understand this speech may have been
written long ago, but the content is very informative and still relevant to this day. We must educate ourselves with as much information as we can to not only increase our welfare of survival but to also
enlighten us on the origin of where many of our fears and pain root
from. I've learned throughout my years on this earth fear and pain
are all part of life, but it can also be inherited as well. Fear of the
unknown is a powerful face of fear.

Apostle Paul said it the best when he talked about how much we
have learned having the potential to confuse us even more.

I communed with mine own heart, saying,
Lo, I am come to great estate, and have gotten
more wisdom than all they that have been before
me in Jerusalem: yea, my heart had great experience of wisdom and knowledge.

And I gave my heart to know wisdom, and
to know madness and folly: I perceived that this
also is vexation of spirit.

For in much wisdom is much grief: and
he that increaseth knowledge increaseth sorrow.
(Ecclesiastes 1:16–18 KJV)

I said in my heart, "I have acquired great
wisdom, surpassing all who were over Jerusalem
before me, and my heart has had great experience
of wisdom and knowledge.

"And I applied my heart to know wisdom and to know madness and folly. I perceived that this also is but a striving after wind.

"For in much wisdom is much vexation, and he who increases knowledge increases sorrow." (Ecclesiastes 1:16–18 ESV)

Review: Obstacles include fear, denial, pain, and confusion, to name just a few. How curious are you regarding how to deal with all this?

The Transition

Life has a very strange way of introducing you to yourself. Whatever is necessary to gain your attention or to correct your steps, God will allow that situation to occur in order to correct you. Look in the mirror and ask yourself, "Are you at where you need to be in your life?"

If that answer is no, then you need to change ASAP. Period! Your life reflects the decisions you have made, and you must take ownership of those decisions. I know it sounds harsh, maybe perplexing, but it's necessary in order for you to change, to transition into a person who questions the status quo in life.

What you see is what you believe. Not true. What you believe is what you see. I will try to help you understand the difference in narratives.

Take a moment. Imagine what your life could've been if you had truly taken those opportunities presented to you. Would you have still run away? In this life, you must be willing to take some risks to succeed. Risks are all a part of life. Chances are, you will fail, but know that, from experience, you are more aware of what it takes to succeed. The knowledge and wisdom gained from failures is a blessing in disguise. Every master was once a student. Life experiences are the professors of the masters classes of life. So stay in school and learn from them.

Time for a movie break!

*****

Long ago, I saw this movie called *The Last Samurai* starring lead actor Tom Cruise as Nathan Algren. There was a scene in which Algren is captured by Katsumoto, leader of the samurai (played by Ken Watanabe), and his army of samurais. Algren is brought back to Katsumoto's village as a POW (prisoner of war).

In the movie, Algren finds himself wandering along the village roads while being heavily watched by a samurai guard. He notices the male samurai of the villages training in the camp. Each one was an expert in their own skills that have been perfected over years of training. Extremely fascinated, Algren got the idea that he himself could get involved in the training. Well, it wasn't exactly like that. He ended up getting forced into the training.

While watching two of the male children practicing with bamboo training swords, one of the children dropped his sword. Out of courtesy, Algren picked up the sword to give it back to the child. This gesture created the opening in which Algren was sucked right into training. He is seen interfering and is commanded by the guards to face one of the young boys in combat training. Algren doesn't take it seriously because it's a child he's up against.

Since Algren was not taking the match seriously enough, an adult male samurai noticed and took much offense. Ujio (played by actor Hiroyuki Sanada), one of Katsumoto's most trusted samurais in the village, decides to step in, so he challenges Algren. This has now become a lesson in humility. Why? It was forbidden to teach outsiders their secret art, especially one who was considered an enemy of their village.

Bear with me. I need you to understand why the mirror analogy I mentioned earlier in chapter 2 matters here as well. The significance of mirror analogy is very important to grasp.

In a matter of seconds, Algren lost the match. The loss of the match lights a fire within Algren's heart. Now he wants to train to not only learn the art but to also redeem himself. Remember this, "Practice makes perfect!"

Ujio and Algren collided several times in the movie. With each confrontation, Ujio noticed Algren had gotten better, unaware that Algren, while still being a prisoner, had found the time to practice improving his skills. Nobutada (played by actor Shin Koyamada), Katsumoto's nephew, intervened in the next battle between Ujio and Algren. This time, Algren got some much-needed advice from the young samurai. This would become the most important advice he would ever get in his entire life. Nobutaba, impulsively eager to help Algren, tells him three important words of advice: "Too many mind."

This statement is in reference to a zen concept known as "no mind." It basically means that you think too much. When tasked with an action, one's mind is on too many things at once, and you cannot concentrate an effort on any one thing. It is a call to relax instead of forcing yourself to think about every move.

*****

This is a notion many of us still suffer from to this day. When we are faced with tough situations, overthinking becomes our go-to defense mechanism. It causes us to drift off, creating unnecessary scenarios to solve our problems.

Back to the movie.

*****

When Algren learned to acknowledge this major flaw, he began to calm his mind and replay everything back in his head. This moment he takes to reflect on all the moves that caused him failures in the battle shatters his own doubts about himself. Once the warriors continue the fight, the results are inevitable. The two mirrored each other's moves to the very last strike, shocking everyone. In disbelief, Ujio bows to Algren as a sign of respect. A transition had occurred.

*****

Now here's my point. Never underestimate the power of the human spirit! *Rupi Kaur* once wrote, "You were born with the weakness to fall. You were born with the strength to rise."

In conquering ourselves, we can change our reality to what we believe it should be. By exploring our own failures, we unlock our own hidden potentials that we are struggling to achieve. As time passes, we can then educate ourselves, feeding that hunger to find the truth about ourselves. There is an old saying I used to hear growing up: "There is no such thing as too much knowledge!"

Over the years, as I've gotten older, I've noticed we have nurtured this belief that mimicking each other is acceptable. At times it can be useful but also detrimental all the same. Without true understanding on when it can be acceptable, it will lead to your major downfall. We must put in the shadow work to developing our own identity and stop adding gasoline to our already flammable insecurities. It's very important that we understand this. In my honest opinion, no one wants to put in that work anymore. We no longer seek individuality, and instead we settle for commonality.

Definition of *commonality*: "the state of sharing features or attributes."

We would rather make excuses on why we can't achieve our goals and accept the circumstances that force us to neglect pursuing our dreams. All we seem to do is watch our dreams being fulfilled through someone else's hard work. Then we have the nerve to try to take credit for what we have yet to master ourselves. It is no wonder why the opinion of others terrifies us.

Our decisions ultimately reveal our biggest fears. Why? Because it's not considered the norm to practice self-discipline. All the greats before us who paved the way knew this one thing: Either you die for something or die for nothing. Now refer back to the question: What are you willing give up?

If you don't surround yourself with individuals who are as driven, loyal, or even atheistic as you, or who chase their dream and not the money, you will always find yourself being a follower of those without. You will be doomed to be a puppet on a string for the rest of your life.

Let that marinate for a while and then ask yourself these questions.

1. When was the last time you truly gave your all into achieving a goal you desired?
2. Was it when you were chasing after a lover you desired to get?
3. Was it when it came to supporting your addictive behaviors?
4. Was it when you realized your children needed food to eat?
5. Was it when you realized you had no one else you could manipulate or depend on?
6. When are you going to do what is necessary in order for you to live and not simply survive?

That list of questions could have gone on and on. That is because transitioning into someone you want to be can vacillate daily. Situations determine what we need to become. Let's move on to how we can survive this ever-changing world.

Survival

We do what is necessary to survive, correct?

This belief is a huge problem. Self-sabotaging is not a natural belief. We must fix our actions by the renewal of our mindsets. Everyone at some point in time has made excuses to justify why changing is so extremely hard. Don't blame yourself. We inherited this trait from those we looked up to or ran to for advice, some of which are still reacting to past traumas yet to be healed.

This is why our children are being suffocated and not developing the skills needed to learn how to swim on their own. We have gotten too comfortable settling, and it needs to stop. Every day, there is a struggle going on within us, but you must not ever forget that you are still blessed. With every new day, you have another chance to fix whatever problems you are facing.

We are blessed in having free will, so utilize it in the correct manner instead of using it for selfish gain. There is no reason why you should be the reason that blocks your own blessings. We must make the necessary changes to transition ourselves into positions that will benefit us to gain the freedom we deserve. It all starts with you.

Stop considering yourself as the victim of your environment and become the victor who conquered it. Focus on knowing God has a plan for you. There are twisted laws that are built to confuse and control you, and they may eventually destroy you.

Right or Wrong or Both?

Look at it this way: what's right is right, and what's wrong is wrong, correct? But what's right could be wrong, and what's wrong could be right! For example, if you see someone who needs assistance crossing the street, the right gesture is to offer your help, correct? Now, same scenario. If you walk past them knowing they could use assistance and do nothing, this can be considered wrong.

Now let's have some fun. Same scenario. What happens if you offer your help to that same individual crossing the street, and that individual completely freaks out and assumes you are trying to rob them? You did the right thing, but the reaction went completely wrong; and now you're arrested for harassment.

You did the right thing, and it turned out wrong; but you can't get mad at them because if you were the one who was old and scared, you may have done the same thing, which would be right to do to protect yourself. It's hard to trust strangers these days. Tell me if I'm lying about this. To be brutally honest with you, it causes great sadness in my heart to even be aware of this misunderstood concept.

Take a moment and examine your past decisions. Ask yourself:

1. Should you or followed the rules all your life?
2. Is it still your fault for what really happened to you in the past?
3. Was following the rules of your parents justifiable for your life now?
4. Should you have sacrificed your dreams to support someone else's dreams and goals?
5. Were you so desperate to be loved, or were you so codependent on having love, you lost yourself? Explain the reason why you feel it's okay to be used and abused, not just physically but emotionally.
6. Should you have saved or invested? (Trust me, there is a difference.)

7. Should you still attend that building with a cross on top we all know as a church? Will it save you from going to hell or not if you never attended?

Side note: I've come to terms with the fact that I've found more devils attending church than on the streets!

Circumstances do not always determine or define your reality, but it sure as hell reveals the possibilities of facing unnecessary circumstances.

Albert Einstein once said, "In matters of truth and justice, there is no difference between large and small problems, for issues concerning the treatment of people are all the same."

During this journey of your healing process, be adaptable in accepting this truth: you will no longer be acceptable to many, but you will be free to be you. You will find that distancing yourself from outside forces may be the only way to stay the course in the development of your growth and self-healing. Not because you want to but because you need to. Friends, family, lovers, even some jobs may need to be reevaluated or cut out completely. If it poses a threat and is a burden to you, *cut it out of your life*!

You will be forced to go into hibernation like bears, isolating yourself for the winter. Don't be afraid of this. This process is designed to help you in the understanding of your own importance and self-development. Much patience will be needed.

Focus—Love

Rejoiceth not in iniquity, but rejoiceth in the truth;

Beareth all things, believeth all things, hopeth all things, endureth all things.

Charity never faileth: but whether there be prophecies, they shall fail; whether there be tongues, they shall cease; whether there be knowledge, it shall vanish away.

For we know in part, and we prophesy in part.

But when that which is perfect is come, then that which is in part shall be done away.

When I was a child, I spake as a child, I understood as a child, I thought as a child: but when I became a man, I put away childish things.

For now we see through a glass, darkly; but then face to face: now I know in part; but then shall I know even as also I am known.

And now abideth faith, hope, charity, these three; but the greatest of these is charity. (1 Corinthians 13:6–13 KJV)

(Love) it does not rejoice at wrongdoing but rejoices with the truth.

Love bears all things, believes all things, hopes all things, endures all things.

Love never ends. As for prophecies, they will pass away; as for tongues, they will cease; as for knowledge, it will pass away.

For we know in part, and we prophesy in part,

but when the perfect comes, the partial will pass away.

When I was a child, I spoke like a child, I thought like a child, I reasoned like a child. When I became a man, I gave up childish ways.

For now, we see in a mirror dimly, but then face to face. Now I know in part; then I shall know fully, even as I have been fully known.

So now faith, hope, and love abide, these three; but the greatest of these is love. (1 Corinthians 13:6–13 ESV)

All my life, I felt as if there was a dark cloud that hovered over me. This made me very resilient on learning how to break free from hell. I sought God in my dreams as I slept more so than when I was awake. Resting was the only peace I knew. My spirit team could talk to me without the distraction of the world. I struggled in finding peace within myself because I didn't love myself.

As I began to focus on what uplifted me, I was able to find the fuel that would ignite that fire again within me. Only then was I able to smile again and stop wearing a mask that only hid myself from me. Thoughts of my sons, my goals, and future dreams began to shine brighter than the morning sun. It uplifted me so much that quitting wasn't an option anymore. Asking God to allow my spirit guides, whom he had tasked over me to protect me, led me to accepting that my ancestors were also there to protect me as well.

God had given me my own spirit team, and together, we became a fierce hurricane, quietly unpredictable. When I struck my target, enemies never saw me coming. That darkness that followed me all those years no longer scared me. In fact, it made me very aware that the devil was after me.

Remember this. If you know the devil is after you, then understand there is something special about you. Figure that out and you will stop running too. When you have been depressed, scared, or angry for so long, nothing will matter after that dysfunctional thinking. "Who can save me?" is the only question that may come to mind. But then another question comes to mind. A very dark question indeed. That is, "Do I even want to be saved?"

Believing in God, nothing else matters. I had never really believed in God or even considered that he existed. But at the lowest point in my life, the Bible was my only true friend. It never lied to me. I found myself, and that's what made me believe in God again. Not some religion, but the very words I read spoke to me. Just because there's a cross on a building doesn't make it a church. In fact, it's a building with a plus sign on top. Didn't the Bible teach us to never place our faith in any graven images?

> Thou shalt not make unto thee any graven image, or any likeness of any thing that is in heaven above, or that is in the earth beneath, or that is in the water under the earth.
>
> Thou shalt not bow down thyself to them, nor serve them: for I the LORD thy God am a jealous God, visiting the iniquity of the fathers upon the children unto the third and fourth generation of them that hate me; and shewing mercy unto thousands of them that love me, and keep my commandments. (Exodus 20:4–6 KJV)

> You shall not make for yourself a carved image, or any likeness of anything that is in heaven above, or that is in the earth beneath, or that is in the water under the earth.
>
> You shall not bow down to them or serve them, for I the LORD your God am a jealous God, visiting the iniquity of the fathers on the children to the third and the fourth generation

of those who hate me, but showing steadfast love
to thousands of those who love me and keep my
commandments. (Exodus 20:4–6 ESV)

This is a battle for souls, and the devil is devising a new weapon.
It's called mind control. If he controls this, your heart will always have
trouble in following what is needed to save your soul. Remember
what I mentioned earlier about the mirror? What you see is what you
believe. That's the devil's trick for the mind. God's plan is to help
learn how to go within; therefore, the devil can't see what you believe,
so what you believe is what you see. That's the secret. Your transition
from dark to light is one focused decision. I choose to get up and
press toward the mark, like Paul said in the Bible (Philippians 3:14).
So tell me, what do you believe?

Wants versus Needs

Mysteries followed by intense discoveries, I must admit, have always been my life.

It seemed as if every day when I woke, my body was already preparing itself for battle. I would lay in my bed and contemplate every event that had already happened to me the day before then strategize my next moves to survive the day at hand. A mentally exhausting period, but I needed to gather my thoughts. Skeptical about everything, all I ever wanted to do was lay back down and do nothing.

I recalled a conversation that I had with my son one morning concerning Christmas. That may have been one of the most serious conversations I ever had in my life. Here's why: at this time, my son was just eleven years old. Somehow, the discussion went from Christmas gifts to me explaining to him the differences between wants and needs.

Follow me. This is going to blow your mind. God can be very funny when he maneuvers in your life to get a particular point across that you have no idea about. Often, he will use anyone or anything to get your attention when doing so. In my case, he used my son to gain my attention. What really intrigued me the most was how he used the conversation my son and I were having and flipped it on me.

During the conversation, I noticed my son's voice had changed. It started to sound as if he was grown, and I was conversing with a grown man. For some strange reason, I began to feel a weird chill come over my body as if I was standing in the freezer with no clothes on. Have you ever been so scared your heart begins to start pounding as if it was going to explode right out of your chest? That was the feeling I felt at that moment.

The presence of a powerful energy from a different world than my own was here, and it was coming right through my own son. Here's how the conversation went.

"Hey, Dad? You want to know something?"

I replied, "Sure, son. What's up?"

He replied, "Gifts are divine purpose. Desires are dangerous. It can lead to actions that can go too far!"

I was completely blown away. First off, who was I really talking to, because this person I was talking to on the phone did not sound like my son at all. And second, where did he get this type of knowledge from? This was no average response given by any eleven-year-old kid. The response was too heavy and thoroughly calibrated together. There wasn't any room for any suspicion or doubt. The response could make you question it, but before you could, you gained the answer.

Only God can do that. A hidden question within an answer but still led you to another question all at the same time. This left me questioning everything about life. Discovering something new can be inspiring but, at the same time, terrifying. What an extremely shocking revelation! The mystery didn't stop there. When I asked my son to repeat himself, his response was, "Huh. Dad, I didn't say that.

What in the world was going on here? That whole day, the echoes of that response replayed in my head. For hours I meditated over what I had just heard. Trying to figure out why, I began to get so frustrated I even took the day off work. Yes, it was that serious. My appetite left me, and rage built up inside of me. All I wanted was to be left alone. This completely disturbed my plans for my day. I prayed and asked God and my spirit's guide to help me understand what I just heard. *What was the reason for this message?* I asked myself.

For hours, I read my Bible, closing it, and then opening it back up repeatedly. Shit, I even googled the response online. Nothing of help could be found. Finally, I had given up trying to solve this riddle. Right then, like a light bulb, a light turned on in my head, and

I thought about a time when Jesus Christ spoke about children and their innocence. In the Book of Isaiah, I found this verse.

> Behold, I and the children whom the LORD hath given me are for signs and for wonders in Israel from the LORD of hosts, which dwelleth in mount Zion. (Isaiah 8:18 KJV)

> Behold, I and the children whom the LORD has given me are signs and portents in Israel from the LORD of hosts, who dwells on Mount Zion. (Isaiah 8:18 ESV)

Listen, I'm more than aware of the verse of this passage referring to something more in depth, but what stuck out the most was when I read the same verse in my other version of the Bible. There was a word that was used, *portents*. This word had replaced *wonders*, which was used in the King James version of the Bible. This made me very cautious.

Definition of *portent*: "a sign or warning that something, especially something momentous or calamitous, is likely to happen."

Definition of *wonders*: "a feeling of surprise mingled with admiration, caused by something beautiful, unexpected, unfamiliar, or inexplicable."

So with this new information, I thought about my son's response once again, but this time I broke into two parts,

- Gifts are divine purpose (*wonders*).
- Desires are dangerous (*portents*). It can lead to actions that can be taken too far."

Did God use my son to deliver a message of warning or comfort? Do you understand now why I took this response from my oldest son so seriously? This was deeper than I thought. Let me pause here for just a moment. Here are a few questions.

More reflection:

1. Do you believe that our young children can be used as instruments of God's divine will?
2. Could our children be more aware of the understanding of both good and evil, even at a young age?
3. Is it safe to say that the younger our children are, the presence of God is more with them than us?

Those words my son spoke to me that day would have changed my whole entire outlook of my life. All my decisions, understanding of situations that ever happened to me, everything that ever gave me pain, and my prospective had changed. Excessively thinking about my life, I began to cry for a very long period of time. A hole in my heart that had never been closed was now filled all due to a child's response.

God had used my son to heal a void that I've always searched for closure from. Things that hunted me were now clear on why it held so much power over my life. Why? Because for many years, I did whatever it took to gain the desires of my heart, but never waiting on God's divine timing to gain the real gifts I needed. So I worked to have the desired things of the heart while trusting I would gain just what I needed. It is true. God will give you what you desire, but is it what you need that will fill the heart.

Recall my earlier credit to the man by the name of Jiddu Krishnamurti. He was an Indian philosopher who taught many around the world of his theory of spirituality. His teaching was unorthodox and copied by none. *He believed that the nature of the mind, meditation, and the radical changes in society were needed to attain total awareness of self. If we misunderstand the events that occurred in the past, we won't learn the lessons needed to help create our futures. We will repeat the same cycles over and over until we have learned the lessons needed to involve becoming better versions of ourselves.*

If we don't change, these cycles will continue. That's why it's known to us as generational curses! We must end these cycles, or our children will be doomed to repeat them. Maybe we should take into consideration that even though these kids may speak very reckless, many of them are crying out for help. We just need to listen more and stop judging them so quickly.

In my case, for a moment my son became my teacher, and I became the student. God works in mysterious ways. So don't tell me God doesn't exist! Reread what my son said to me and ask yourself, "How I would feel if my child spoke to me in the same manner?"

The Crossroads

Choices. How unbelievably complicated they are to comprehend. Yes. No. Right. Wrong etc.

Life can be very simple yet so complex at times. Sometimes we must take into consideration that the avenues we embark upon during our journeys can cause much heartache and pain. These intense situations we often face dictate much of our implosive attitudes.

Remember the example, "sometimes doing the right things could be wrong, and doing the wrong things could be right"? Doing the right thing could explode a simple situation into a brawl. Freewill is as much of a burden as believing in yourself. You must change the narrative and dig deeper than you ever dug to find the strength to overcome obstacles hindering you from moving forward in life. If not, you will wind up placing a dagger into your own back. Take the risk of learning how to solve your own problems instead of always looking for help. You are your own best therapist.

Isaac Newton once's said, "For every action, there is an equal and opposite reaction."

Ask yourself these three major questions:

1. What are you willing to give up in order to achieve your highest dreams?
2. If you had to lose everything, could you live with the choices?
3. Could you accept death as an outcome to protect your dream?

Everything in this world costs something, and you must be aware of that. To maintain the balance in your life, you must consider the pros and cons of every thought and action.

> I press toward the mark for the prize of the high calling of God in Christ Jesus.
>
> Let us therefore, as many as be perfect, be thus minded: and if in anything ye be otherwise minded, God shall reveal even this unto you.
>
> Nevertheless, whereto we have already attained, let us walk by the same rule, let us mind the same thing. (Philippians 3:14–16 KJV)

> I press on toward the goal for the prize of the upward call of God in Christ Jesus.
>
> Let those of us who are mature think this way, and if in anything you think otherwise, God will reveal that also to you.
>
> Only let us hold true to what we have attained. (Philippians 3:14–16 ESV)

No matter what happens in our lives, we must always push forward. It can be terrifying at times, but staying in the dark can be a lot worse. Facing the extremities of life is necessary to grow. Every moment you face in which life knocks you down are usually the best teachers. These lessons are meant to help you learn, improve, and find the inner strength to stand up and believe in yourself all over again.

Don't be surprised if you begin to say to yourself, "I can, and I won't give up!"

We often underestimate ourselves way too much, and that too must stop. The real issue is, why must we go through all the hell to understand this? There are many who are aware and are beginning to notice that the masks that they wear are no longer keeping them safe from reality. In fact, it keeps them blinded from the truth. All we keep hearing is, "God is coming back, and soon all this suffering will end!"

Don't worry, I'll say it for you. "When is that supposed to happen, because I'm getting sick and tired of hearing this!"

Many of us are getting sick and tired of going to church because we can't even trust the people in them anymore. We are getting sick and tired of praying, hoping, and believing in someone who we are all confused about. I mean, the list can go on! Correct? Sometimes you have to let it all out because if you don't and let it bottle up inside, it will kill you! There's a common saying I believe we all have heard before: "Life is a game that must be played!"

News flash! *Life is not a game!* You can't hit restart, and you can't save your spot on where you left off. People are spiritually dying left and right, and it seems nobody truly cares about it. "If it doesn't make money, it doesn't make sense." Isn't that the motto we all hear now? We really need to become more optimistic if our future has even a chance of survival. Right now, no one can decipher the sheep from the wolves anymore. Why? Because the wolves are no longer hiding behind the door. We have invited them into our own homes, and here's the twist. Some of us are sleeping with them.

We are exposing ourselves to danger, and we have gotten too comfortable in doing so. The fork in the road is not a myth. There is no in-between; you either go left or right, because going straight only means you lack discernment and would rather take a shortcut to victory, becoming more naïve to the idea that you must take responsibility for your actions. What's the use of gaining wisdom if you lack the knowledge to use it correctly.

It hurts to see so many of our people lost and accepting it! But what really hurts the most is that many have taken their own lives because this harsh truth is hard to deal with. Many had cried out for help in their own way, but we neglected to notice the signs. What happened to having real compassion for one another? Why is it wrong to have a heart and show genuine love for each other? We are so broken inside we can never even realize that the light of others is not out; it's just low, and all that is needed is a little more fuel to have it burn bright once again.

Everyone faces a crossroad at some point in their lives. Some just get stuck, and all these individuals are waiting for is someone who is willing to take a chance on them so they can understand the path that is in front of them. If you have the experience that can help them along their journey, it is your responsibility to share it; if not, their blood will be on your hands, like it or not. Tell them, "You're not alone."

I understand reading this may hurt or even remind you of past traumas you wish to forget, but it's needed to understand where this rage you keep inside all started from. Neglecting those whom you can help is as bad as having a child then putting them up for adoption. I had to face this truth myself, and it almost broke me as well.

My faith carried me through it all because if I didn't believe in God, I would have given up a long time ago or, even worse, would have become the murderer of one of you all. No one came to my rescue when I asked for help. Many didn't understand me, nor did they want to help me. They would stare and point their finger at me and laugh like my circumstances were a joke, or in response to my plight, they would offer some type of illegal substance that it will help ease my mind.

I'm here now—all praise be unto God—and want to let everyone who had done this that I'm glad I had the courage to let you go. I was willing to walk this path of healing alone. Sometimes it can be better that way. Toxic people can only blind you from accepting the truth that you must change to set yourself free from the hell you feel trapped in.

One thing I can promise you is, you will make it through it even if you must do it alone. But remember, you are not alone, so don't give up! We are warriors, kings, and queens of the Most High. Your ancestors and spirit guides, who are tasked by God himself to watch over you, are always near you. Don't be afraid to take a chance on yourself. Know you are worth it! Remember, you will never change anything if you are not willing to put the work in, so I guess you better do it now while you have the strength or accept the inevitability of becoming another statistic!

The greatest breakthrough in life is *self-discovery*. Until you face yourself, you will always seek to become someone else. Listen to that inner voice inside you that tells you, "You can achieve it. Keep going. You're almost there."

Stop running from yourself. The time is now, so stand up! Lace up your boots, grab your things, begin walking out of that dark abyss called pain, straighten up your back, and stand tall. You are the light in the dark. Know that this world needs you to succeed. God needs you to succeed. Your children and your loved ones need you to succeed. You may be the only one in the family that can break that generational curse that hovers over you and the family before and after you.

Take pride in knowing that what you're going through right now may lay the foundation that the lost souls on this earth need to walk on to return their faith back into believing in God again. Hold your head high so they can see you. If you understand this, then you were chosen to be a part of God's new army. Act like you got some sense and choose love. God's angels are at our side, willing and ready to put some work in—are you? When you reach that crossroad, put those critical-thinking skills to use and choose.

The Breakthrough

As I reflect on all that I had to experience in my life, becoming a prisoner of my own mind was the last thought I could ever believe.

The idea that I could be exposed to lingering thoughts outside of my control seemed to always disturb me. What the eyes see, the mind believes, correct? And for every action, there's an opposite and equal reaction. The more time I spent pondering about this, I found one thing was certain. Old habits had to die to develop new habits to survive.

Many nights, I would stay awake reflecting on how my life could've been if I took more time strategizing on how to improve myself instead of overthinking about situations I couldn't control. If it's meant to be, it will be, right? This made me ask myself a huge question, "Why do we push ourselves so hard to keep things that we know aren't good for us?"

Being vulnerable can be a blessing and a curse, especially when your actions don't align with the steps needed to head toward your purpose.

Long ago I wrote a poem call "Miseries." This poem was supposed to help me release the stress I was feeling at that time, but it wound up becoming the catalyst that helped me discover myself. Poetry was an outlet for me growing up as a young kid. It forced me to examine myself in a positive way, without the worries of being judged by anyone. It also taught me how to be patient in understanding my thoughts fully. Maybe that's why I love jigsaw puzzles so much. The idea that a huge mess can become a masterpiece always fascinated me.

Here is the poem. I hope it resonates with you.

Remember, this is how I felt then, and trust me, it was a very dark time.

Miseries

written by, Robert Zadkiel Young

So much pain, I'm so confused. Hatred clouds my soul, and I'm unsure how to move on. So many demons trying to control me; I'm losing faith on how to hold on. I'm going astray, Lord. Why don't you speak to me? Darkness is all around me; I'm blinded by this cage in front of me. Forgive me, Lord, if I missed the signs. You made me this way, so on you I place the blame. All you do is watch from afar, don't you have wings? Is my life supposed to be a game to you?

Evil people are being blessed, but here I am, stressed, leaning on the wall. It's cold where I am; no sun, no warmth in the air. The more I climb, the more I fall. It's plain to see that we call you Lord, but it's the landlords who oversee. Has He turned away from me? Were my evil deeds too much to see? I was told you hold the masterplans, but as my life unfolds, that's hard to believe. I turn my head to the east; still, I find no peace. All I see are burning flames consuming my dreams.

Why should I care and put my faith in a cross? Destined to die, who would remember me. So leave me be and move on. It's okay. In fact, erase me. It's not like you took time to teach me. I tried my best to believe; all I received was another reason to hate you. All I wanted was for you to notice me, hold me, and be a friend to me. Instead you left me alone to be abused and used by people who hated me.

87

It must feel good to be a God. You have no one to answer to. Some God you are, creating puppets just to keep you amused.

If I die, let these be my last words I'll ever say to you.

Thank you for leaving me. I know now I never meant nothing to you.

Socrates once said, "True wisdom comes to each of us when we realize how little we understand about life, ourselves, and the world around us."

There is a difference between knowledge and wisdom. You study to gain knowledge, but you must have understanding of that knowledge to gain wisdom. If you don't understand this, be prepared to endure much sorrow and pain. There are levels in life you must pass in order to graduate. Some pass, others barely make it, and then there's those who just fail it. This is the harsh truth, and it's a very hard pill to swallow.

This journey can be very troublesome, but it must be lived out. So many roads can lead to your downfall. Although this may cause much sadness, we must continue to proceed. Only now, we must do it with caution. Signs are shown all around us to help us along the way. It is just hard to see them when you have a tainted faith.

I've learned that whenever you lose your way, your God himself has always been there to direct you. We choose to be impatient when the answers are right there in your face. Yes, angels do exist, but they are not allowed to intervene in the way you want them to because this will be breaking God's rules. To intervene in someone's freewill is a huge issue when comes to obeying spiritual laws.

Angels can guide you, but they must place their trust more into you following your intuition. They can only guide you. It's a soft voice when you hear it, very subtle yet peaceful and strong. That's your guardian angel speaking to you. So listen carefully. That's how they operate. Now be very mindful: the devil can operate in the same manner. Remember, he was once the angel of light as well. I can't stress it enough: you must stay up in prayer to truly understand this.

Definition of *intuition*: "the ability to understand something immediately, without the need for conscious reasoning; a thing that one knows or considers likely from instinctive feeling rather than conscious reasoning."

Whenever you are scared, lost, or afraid, know you're never alone. Many nights, I would just walk outside and just stare at the night skies, watching the stars, asking God to send me a best friend. It's strange, but I would always hear a voice saying, "I'm right here with you!"

It's a comforting feeling yet so overwhelming. It's as if you are being covered by large wings that are as soft as a pillow yet so strong, as if a shield clothed around you. Sometimes I would take runs to the waterfront because I knew deep down in my heart the farther I went, the more angels had to run after me just to keep me safe from harm.

As I rested at night, I would thank them for putting up with my crazy self and hope to wake up to feel their presence again. It felt as if all of them were surrounding me, touching me, rejuvenating my soul and energy so I could do it all over again. We must understand whenever we are lost in our minds, all we have to do is rest a bit and ask our guides to help us. That's all. Leave the rest to God. Trust me. They hear you, and they have a very funny sense of humor. Well, some. They can be very serious as well. Don't ever mistake that. They are here to protect you. Do not play around with them. The mind and the spirit will work all on its own, giving you all the information needed to understand this.

I know I said I felt alone in my younger years, but I have come to realize that I wasn't alone. Not really. I'm guessing the demons were hovering closely too in my darker times. Your angelic hosts were there too, but their energy differs. It's unmistakable to know now. I feel if we all understood this, we would smile more and love each other better. It's okay to cry and ask for help when people are doing you wrong. Just know they are being watched; trust me when I say that. They will suffer for what they have done to you, and the best part is, they won't even see it coming.

When God reacts, trust and believe you will be there to witness the horrifying vengeance done on behalf of you. God will ensure your enemies know he is the Lord. He will get the glory, punishing all those who ever had done wrong to his children. Make no mistake. No evil deeds done in the dark will go unjustified. Read Proverbs 11–21.

> Though hand join in hand, the wicked shall not be unpunished: but the seed of the righteous shall be delivered. (Proverbs 11:21 KJV)

> Be assured, an evil person will not go unpunished, but the offspring of the righteous will be delivered. (Proverbs 11:21 ESV)

When you hurt one of God's chosen earth angels, the heavens will open and, with his majesty, fire will rain down. Take heed to what I am saying to you please. Laugh if you want. God can put an end not just to you but to your entire bloodline after to you, just because of a mistake you own. Oh yes, the heavens take great offense to any transgression that can affect a future generation. That's why punishment from God is felt through the ages. Does Adam and Eve ring a bell? Aren't we still paying for their disobedience?

There are twenty-four Bible verses that talk about how the sins of the father will visit future generations. Study that on your own for a minute. Take a look at Exodus 20:5–6, which says, "…visiting the iniquity of the fathers upon the children unto the third and fourth generation of them that hate me and showing mercy unto thousands of them that love me," for a start to your own studies. Then move on to include Ezekiel 18:20 and Deuteronomy 24:16. The computer can make your search and study easier but be careful of false prophets in the interpretation.

No one will get away from what they have done to you. You just got to have the strength to endure the troubling times and watch and see how fast God works in your life. This truth is not even taught to most of us. Many couldn't comprehend the effect transgression can do to you and your children's children. Understand something, this isn't only about you. This is more than you can ever fathom. What you go through in life is to test you to see if you are worthy of the crown God will bestow upon you.

It was never just about good and evil. Remember, God is building an army of chosen ones to stand by his side. Did you get that? I'll say it again. God is building a new army of chosen ones too stand by his side in battle. That means God will fight alongside of you, and with your very eyes, you will see the true power of our King in all his majesty. Full of glory.

"Behold, I come quickly." From my favorite, Book of Revelations, specifically Revelations 22:12, which says, "And behold, I come quickly; and my reward is with me, to give every man according as his work shall be."

Throughout the Bible, mention is made of God's return to earth to dole out justice "as a thief in the night," "in the twinkling of an eye," swiftly he comes. Also check out 1 Corinthians 15:52, which says, "In a moment, in the twinkling of an eye, at the last trump: for the trumpet shall sound and the dead shall be raised incorruptible, and we shall be changed."

Isn't that what the Lord promises us? He reveals to us that he will come like a thief in the night. No one will know when he'll come. There's no need to think about whether he will show up in the sky. The truth of the matter is, God has been here all along! We just don't know it! The ground beneath our feet makes it seem as if we are on solid ground, but you misunderstood what Scriptures says.

> "Thus," saith the LORD, "The heaven is my throne, and the earth is my footstool: where is the house that ye build unto me? and where is the place of my rest?" (Isaiah 66:1 KJV)

> "Thus" says the LORD: "Heaven is my throne, and the earth is my footstool; what is the house that you would build for me, and what is the place of my rest?" (Isaiah 66:1 ESV)

Did you catch it? That's why he promises to never leave you. He is waiting on us; we are the house getting built, but until the building is done, we won't rest. So he's always up, wondering and watching everything we do. Once the house is built and cleaned up, then he will rest, and so will you!

Seeking Purpose

Finding your purpose in life is very important! The idea of misunderstanding the steps that must be taken can be very emotional and harsh all at the same time. After all that has been written here in this book—sharing my experiences on what I've learned throughout the process—still, all I can do is reflect on all that I had to give up just to reach this point in my life.

Through many of my childish actions, habits, and even beliefs, I understand now more than ever it wasn't worth the pain I caused many along the way. When you are seeking your purpose in this life, you must reflect on all that you have gone through and try your hardest to understand everything. All that life will throw at you will break you in ways that will make even the strongest person cry. Loving people will hurt, relationships will seem to never go right, and trusting in many people will simply be a mission all on its own. Yet it is necessary to face your demons, no matter what. Sacrifices are needed if you ever wish to walk this path and live through it,

Everything that you have gone through led to this very moment in your life. This very moment may never come again, so you must stay vigilant and aware of the signs when they are presented to you to understand the pain I'm speaking about; you had to have lost everything at least once in your life.

Life will always be a mystery. We live in a world in which the impossible is possible, and many can contest to that being the absolute truth. Your dreams don't have to be dreams. If you believe in them hard enough your faith can make it reality. There is a word for this concept. It's called *manifestation.*

Whatever your desires in your heart, all you have to do is ask God for it. He will direct your steps in order to achieve whatever that is. Believe in yourself enough to know that all God wants is to make you happy. But you must prove to God that you deserve it. Why? It wouldn't make sense to God to give you something you ask for when he knows you can't handle it.

One thing I've learned is that God watches other things in your life in order to bless you according to his will and plans for you. Your dreams and plans must align with your purpose.

Material gain, family, etc. I mean everything. It is only at your lowest point does the need for a better life truly begin to matter. Living a peaceful life has always been the purpose many of us seek, but having to be submissive to something greater to you is the real test. The idea that you must bow down to something greater than you is perplexing, but aren't your dreams worth bowing to? Is not trusting in God worth it? We must honestly ask ourselves these questions every day.

Definition of *perplexing*: "completely baffling; very puzzling."

Once you reach this part of your life, days and nights no longer seem the same at all. In fact, to be very honest, you may not even know the differences at all. The more you feed your soul with positive affirmations, the more the soul will crave it.

Examples of positive affirmations are: visualize your dreams and goals. There is a method called a vision board. It doesn't have to be a large board, but it should be large enough for your post on your wall or mirror where you will see it every day. On this board, paste pictures of where you want to be and what you want to do. Your heart's desires. Are they in-line with your purpose? Write down your positive affirmations too. Always remember that your vision won't be just handed to you. You must work for it.

Here are some examples of positive affirmations:

1. I am brave enough to overcome obstacles that come my way.
2. I will never be poor again.

3. I will succeed and do good so that blessings continue to follow me.
4. My dream will come to reality as long as I stay focused and keep the faith.
5. I am good enough!
6. I will never give up on myself.
7. I'm a winner. I deserve to be a winner!

Plan what you need to do to reach those goals. Be aware. Anything else will become a distraction. Your old ways of thinking will change, and it will become easier for you to let your past go. Once you make the decision to change, I will advise you to prepare yourself for a battle like no other. Life is going to throw everything at you to test your loyalty to this change.

Emotions can blind you, and wearing your heart on your sleeve won't work. Your enemies come from every corner. Some, you will know, and others you won't even see coming; but you must stay strong throughout it all. You will feel betrayed, hurt, sad, or angry if the thought of hurting someone or yourself plagues your mind. Trust the process. It all has a reason for why it happens. This is why the Bible teaches us:

> For many are called, but few are chosen.
> (Matthew 22:14 KJV)

> For many are called, but few are chosen.
> (Matthew 22:14 ESV)

No explanation needed. When you are called, will you be worthy? Did you put enough work into yourself to be chosen?

Along your journey, many will not be able to go with you, and that's the harsh truth. You alone heard the call, and unless God deems it to be that others know, he would have let them know for you. You alone will have to bear your cross. Trust me when I tell you this, your life will not be the same, but know this too: it is a part of God's plan for your life. This is the part many hate to understand.

Why must this happen to me?

You may tell yourself, "Well, it's the only way to protect you from the snakes that are already crawling in your backyard." God must bring them out to view in order for them to be exposed so you can fight them in the way he wants you to. Eventually, he will destroy them, but he must reveal them to you so you won't ever have to question him on why. You are precious to God, and he will protect you at any cost. Hence, the real reason why we have angels assigned to protect us.

Yes, they are here to protect us, but understand that they do God's biddings according to his will as well. Know they are your spiritual assassins, as well if need be. If you ever read the book *The Art of War*, you will know the best way to destroy the enemy is not solely by attacking them. You must control their resources, in which lies their hearts. Like I mentioned before in this book, if anyone does harm to any of God's children, trust me, they will pay for it, even if it's with their own lives.

Have you ever known anyone who moves in silence to tell everyone their plans? No. Only foolish people do that. The God we serve is not a fool but a true master strategist. God has a plan for your life, but many of us forget that because life can make it seem otherwise, we doubt him because of this. This can cause many of us to go into depression or suffer from severe illness.

PTSD

Let me share this as well.

When I left the Marines in 2014, a few years later, I noticed a dramatic change in my sleep patterns. My body seemed out aligned. This made me very concerned. The very next day I decided to reach out to the Va and set up an appointment with Mental health for veterans. After explaining to the nurse some of my issues I was assigned a psychologist. During my visit I explained that I was waking up in cold sweats and at times completely unaware where I was at. Having bad dreams from combat situations I was in etc. After a few more visit, counseling sessions the final diagnosis showed that I had signs of PTSD. To be very honest, after all that I had been through in my life, I just felt I had anger issues, or abandonment issues, etc. From what I learned, post-traumatic stress disorder was part of life. At least, part of my life lessons. Here is what I decided about this label they gave me after i decided to do my own studies & research on the syndrome.

I realized I had already had the signs of having this curse ever since birth and never even knew it. Let me address something here before you lose your mind. PTSD is a symptom and not a disorder as many believe. This curse can be triggered by anything, but in most cases, we believe only those who have served in the military and fought in wars are the ones who have it. That is false, and I'll prove it!

If you experience any violent situations or traumatizing events in your life, you suffer from PTSD. Remember, it's a symptom, not a disease.

Definition of *PTSD* (post-traumatic stress disorder): "a disorder in which a person has difficulty recovering after experiencing or witnessing a terrifying event."

Any events that occurred in your life can and will trigger this disorder. Why? Because it has to do with the physical effects on the mind which, in turn, affects your emotions. When you have a mental breakdown, your emotional wellbeing is affected because of the trauma. This can be caused by loneliness, codependency issues, alcohol, bad relationships, divorce, being raised in a broken home, absence of mother or father or both, the military, insomnia, etc. So when you point the finger at those who suffer from this, just remember you got three other figures pointing right back at you.

When pursuing your purpose in life, you will face similar triggers, so don't be naïve. You see, psychiatrists won't tell you this. Most will listen to you vent and give you some advice, but others will be quick to end the discussion with their opinion and advice that sounds like this, "Have you consider taking medication to help you?"

Am I wrong? Medicines are only temporary fixes that only suppress the emotions when triggered and does not treat the actual disorder itself. PTSD is not self-inflicted. It is caused by being exposed to harsh if not unexpected conditions or events that occur in your life. As a result your emotion becomes imbalanced and you suffer from what we all know as (Fight or Flight) moments. A response in which the body's natural defense mechanism is highly alerted in response in trying to protect itself. This condition is deemed destructive to others or even to the patient themselves. Any individual who suffers from PTSD will automatically scare others, and this is why it's such a sensitive topic to speak on. So, why take any risk after hearing some of these veterans or civilian stories. Let's medicate them, let's control them.

Many Psychologists presume from the moment you begin to express what's going on there is a high percentage that you need medication. "Here is a prescription for some pills. Call us back if you need to follow up or any refill." Does this sound familiar?

Some situations don't require medicines and the doctors know that. More Counseling maybe, but in many cases better support!

Male/female Group counseling is amazing in my opinion; very effective. Having a legitimate support system can do wonders, trust me. But is this taken seriously no; why? Veterans like myself are just dollar signs! This is why many vets don't receive all the proper help needed. You gotta keep the money flowing.

So, in many cases patients get addicted to the drugs given to them. The truth of the matter is, when these drugs can no longer help other drugs, stronger drugs are sought after. This is usually when things get out of hand and unfortunately things get out of control and we begin to lose many at a rapid rate. The term PTS will never get used. This is why the term PTSD (Post-Traumatic Syndrome Disorder) is used. It's marketable. This is not just my opinion; this is the honest truth. look around you, can't you see it for yourself?

Finding Purpose

Sorry, that needed to be said. Let's get back on topic.

Seeking purpose! When you decide to take a leap of faith on yourself, a lot will be revealed. Everyone has a unique purpose in life. You can try to act the same as everyone else, but a copycat cannot make the same impact as the original.

God adjusts our path according to his will and not your own. When you let expectations go, you will see how unnecessary they are to have. Why? Expectations consist of having limits which you were never born to have. All that matters is divine timing. Your purpose will be revealed to you when you come to the age of understanding.

"Age is nothing but a number." Sorry, but that's a false statement!

Stop living your dreams through someone else's life. Living your life is hard enough. I'm a proud father of two boys. The last thing I want for my kids are bills and questions like, "Why couldn't Dad plan his life better if he loved us?"

There's a burning fire within us all, so change. Change for your kids, change for those who you want to be there, change for yourself, change for God! Because he needs you too! Look at me now, I'm a book author, Marine, and spiritual coach, a father who is still in his kid's lives. Yes, that does matter! I'm very proud of myself, and I'm not looking back.

So tell your story, spread the word that God has placed in your heart. God is real, and he does believe in you. Your story has just begun. Don't you see the light? It's not a train: it's the end of the tunnel, and the light is the Son. Life is not just about watching other people live while you sit and stare. Life is about manifesting your dreams into reality so that one day you can live it instead of dreaming about it.

Acknowledgments

I'm very grateful and humble to have been exposed to so many people's lives while growing up. The lessons that were taught, the stories that were told, all made an impact on my life. Lessons of humility, forgiveness, love, and even regrets gave me the encouragement to stand on my own two feet and become my own man.

To the *mothers of my children*. I'm very grateful for you both. Strong Black, African American queens. Very driven and loving in their own ways. Thank you, ladies. We have had many ups and downs, but in the end, it was all worth it. Thank you for dealing with my crazy self. Thank you for being the queens that you are and holding it down no matter what. Most importantly, thank you for giving me the greatest gifts God can could have ever given me through you both, and those are my sons, Bryson Emmanuel Young and Kiro Isiah young. If I could leave anything more important than money, this would be it. My story and my legacy. I love you, my sons. May God always shine on you both and your mothers.

To *my mother* who played a major role in my life. You are my best friend. We went through hell and back, and still we made it. You are my backbone; there are no greater words to describe you than that. I guess the myth is true. It does take a village to raise a kid because we needed everyone when the ones who were supposed to be there turned their backs on us. God took care of us. Now let them witness with their own eyes.

"Look at my son now! Author and a United States Marine. Eat your heart out."

I'm a product of the people. My life was hell, but I walked through it like a boss and sat in the boss' chair. My God runs this here. All praise goes unto God YAHAWA. I gained a lot of great friends and some enemies, too, but it's all good.

Everyone has their part to play in your life and accept it. So what is your story? You now know mine. We can talk all day to each other and still won't make an impact on each other. Only by sharing our issues, relatable pains, and struggles are we able to do this. So hold on and stay strong. I'm ready to read yours. Are you?

References

Note: All Bible citations come from the King James Version or the English Standard version of the Holy Bible.

Amy Marschall, PsyD. Published on October 11, 2021, reviewed by David Susman, PhD: https://www.verywellmind.com/the-four-fear-responses-fight-flight-freeze-and-fawn-5205083
Medically reviewed by Lori Lawrenz, PsyD—By Beth Ann Mayer on July 27, 2021: https://www.healthline.com/health/mental-health/shadow-work